TOP GUN

THE SECRETS OF
RELATIONSHIP BASED SELLING

FINANCIAL SERVICE EDITION

By
Scott Magnacca, CFP®

authorHOUSE®

AuthorHouse™
1663 Liberty Drive
Bloomington, IN 47403
www.authorhouse.com
Phone: 1-800-839-8640

Published by AuthorHouse 7/05/2012

ISBN: 978-1-4184-0118-4 (sc)
ISBN: 978-1-4184-0119-1 (e)

Library of Congress Control Number: 2004106996

DISCLOSURE

Note: Some Military Photographs and imagery in this book came from DOD DefenseLINK (http://www.defenselink.mil) and were available in the public domain at the time of publication. Photographs and imagery on DefenseLINK, unless otherwise noted, are in the public domain.

The military photographs used in this publication are being used courtesy of the United States Department of Defense. Every effort has been made to determine if any of these photos are subject to copy write and no ownership, other that the above, could be established at the time of publication.

DISCLAIMER

The views and opinions expressed by the author are his own individually and do not in any way reflect or represent the views of any specific investment, insurance, banking or financial services firm on the subject matter discussed.

Neither the author, nor the publisher can be held responsible for any direct or incidental loss incurred by applying any of the information offered. The information provided is meant to be general in nature and should not be considered legal, tax or investment advice. *Please consult your own tax, legal, compliance or financial advisor for additional information concerning the concepts discussed and how they may or may not apply to your specific situation.* The author and publisher specifically disclaim all responsibility for any liability, loss or risk, personal or otherwise, which may be incurred as a consequence, directly or indirectly, by the use or application of any of the contents of this book.

DEDICATION

This book is dedicated to my wife, Dr. Sharon Treston-Magnacca and my three children Treston, Connor and Ryan. I am thankful and honored to have you as a part of my life.

And to you the reader.

The strategies and techniques in this book are simple-but not simple-minded. They are powerful and effective, yet simple to understand, use and apply.

Top marketing and sales professionals, leading politicians, law enforcement, religious leaders and successful entrepreneurs and managers are using many of these same strategies *right now* to improve their relationship building skills and to increase their influence, sales skills and overall effectiveness.

You can too.

In fact, this information can be used and applied in any business or activity –personal and professional- that involves influencing, persuading and communicating with other people.

Consider this. If you aren't using and applying this type of information in your personal or business life right now, chances are, your competition is.

ACKNOWLEDGEMENTS

I am grateful to a great number of people that I have met during the last two decades in my personal and professional life who have directly and indirectly contributed to the development of the content and ideas for this book.

To my brother Mark Magnacca. The technologies, ideas and sales strategies that we discovered and learned together over many years continue to amaze and surprise me in their simplicity, effectiveness and impact.

To the leaders, past and present, in the fields of sales excellence, personal coaching, management development, business, media and politics. Tony Robbins, Zig Ziglar, Napoleon Hill, Steven Covey, Peter Drucker, Tom Peters, Dr. Robert Cialdini, Warren Buffett, Bill Gates, Oprah Winfrey, Ted Turner, Ronald Reagan, John F. Kennedy, Martin Luther King, Bill Clinton and the dozens of other leaders in our society past and present that have made a difference and made an impact in their own unique way.

I respect and admire your business acumen, your communications and persuasion skills and your *passion* to win.

To my colleagues in the Financial Services industry and especially to Farrell Dolan, my friend and mentor in the retirement income planning world. Your passion and enthusiasm for what you do is second to none.

To the "TOP GUN" wholesalers I have met in recent years in the mutual fund, managed account and insurance industries.

You realize that it's *not enough* to just sell the product features and benefits of your specific mutual fund, annuity or managed account.

You know that product features can and will be quickly copied and replicated if they are successful in the marketplace, therefore you add value to your relationships in ways that don't just revolve around products, features and benefits.

And finally, to the TOP GUN financial advisors. Your among the 'best of the best' at what you do. You have worked hard over the years, trained extensively and put what you have learned to work in the real world. You've built your business by helping clients solve their important financial challenges—and you realize that even though your business may be doing well today, you always need to keep current and maintain the winners edge. You realize there is always another level to reach for.

Although the products you sell are for the most part *exactly the same* as the products sold by the other 650,000 licensed brokers in the marketplace today, you have learned to *differentiate yourself and your company* in a way that creates interest in your services and drives clients to *want to* do business with you.

As a result, industry research shows that your sales, revenues and profits for your practice average approximately ***ten times*** that of the "average" advisor.

The secret to your success?

- You have learned, practiced and mastered the techniques and strategies that have allowed you to **focus your time and efforts** in the areas where you will receive the **most payoff.**
- You have learned to **position and market yourself** the right way, to the right people and the right time and **to specialize** in a **growing segment** of the marketplace.
- You have learned how to **effortlessly and effectively communicate** your unique value proposition to your ideal clients and prospects.
- You have learned how to **quickly engage and motivate** both clients and prospects so that they will want to *take action* and buy from you.

In the coming pages, just like in the Navy's TOP GUN program, we will share your secrets of success, and we will learn many new secrets and strategies that are being used effectively right now by some of the most successful salespeople in the industry.

At the most basic level, every wholesaler and every financial advisor who is serious about his or her profession realizes over time the importance of the four principals noted above. We are NOT in the business of just selling products. Anyone can do that. We are in the business of finding customer wants and needs, **building relationships** and making investor dreams a reality. That's where the value added happens. The product sales that come after the relationship is developed are the way we execute on a well-crafted financial plan.

I have a question for you. What is the one thing that all of your prospects and clients need but don't yet have? What's the one thing that they need to make sure that they 'arrive successfully' at retirement? Well, as you know, one of the biggest dreams and most important needs that *virtually every* investor has is being able to enjoy the lifestyle that they want at retirement. This is the pot of gold at the end of the rainbow for every investor.

As investment professionals, the challenge we all face is that *without specialized help* and *without a detailed, personalized written <u>retirement income plan</u>* many of our clients retirement dreams will remain unfulfilled. This book will show you how to profit by targeting the right people at the right time with the right offer and enable you to transform your business by becoming an expert in the retirement income planning marketplace

The coming decades will present those in the financial services business with the opportunity of a lifetime. The question is, how many financial advisors will be properly trained, ready and willing to provide the retirement income services that clients need most?

For those that are prepared, there is no better business to be in-- and no better time to be in it than right now.

Once you learn these techniques and practice them, they will become automatic and habitual and part of the way you naturally do business.

Most importantly, you will learn how to communicate and *sell more effectively* with *less time* and *less overall effort* than you may have dreamed possible before.

Let's begin!

TABLE OF CONTENTS

Chapter5: Winning Sales Tactics During the Appointment

Chapter6: Retirement Income Referrals-Your 'Force Multiplier'

Conclusion: Mission Debriefing

PART ONE

CAPITALIZING ON THE RETIREMENT INCOME REVOLUTION

Following the light of the sun, we left the Old World

-Christopher Columbus

Introduction

What lies behind us and what lies before us are small matters compared to what lies within us.

-Ralph Waldo Emerson

Christopher Columbus was one of the greatest salespeople in history. We learn about him in grade school, but we don't give him nearly enough credit.

Without his sales, influence and persuasion skills, chances are that you and I would not be living- and the United States would not exist.

The world would be a very different place than it is today.

During his youth, Columbus was an avid sailor and spent a considerable amount of time near the sea. During his teenage years, he became an avid reader and went into business as a map maker.

During his early years, one book that he read changed his life forever. It changed his beliefs about what was possible and got him thinking about devoting his time to doing something great, something significant with his life.

The book was written by Marco Polo, the great explorer of the 12th century who wrote a book entitled *The Travels of Marco Polo.*

This book inspired Columbus to believe that he could actually reach the Indies by traveling west instead of east.

At the time, this was a preposterous point of view. No one thought it could be done. It was simply impossible.

Many veteran sailors of the day still believed that the world was flat and that if they sailed too far they might fall of the end of the earth.

Columbus didn't believe the conventional wisdom of the day. He thought differently.

He was convinced that with the proper navigational skill and training -- and with the right crew he could accomplish his mission of discovery.

Unfortunately, other than his belief in his ability, he didn't have any money, any ships or any crew to help him. That didn't stop him, however.

Columbus believed, like all great salesmen, that one could always find enough money and enough resources *if your offer is compelling enough and the payoff is big enough.*

Columbus made his first few proposals to the King of Portugal, the King of France and the King of England. He was quickly rejected out of hand each time.

After thinking for some time about this rejection, he realized that during his presentations he was talking all about *what* he would do and *how* he would do it, but that he had neglected to answer the most important unspoken question. He needed to explain **why** he wanted to do this journey and what benefit it would offer to his supporters. As a result, he realized that he needed to spend more time improving and refining his pitch and his overall presentation.

Each time he was rejected, Columbus learned what *not to do* the next time. Before his presentation to the King and Queen of Spain, he shut himself away in a room for days and worked diligently on improving his presentation.

He considered all the possible objections.
He thought about things from the King's perspective rather than his own.

He thought about his own internal motivation and why he was motivated to do this, despite the risk and personal sacrifices and why he was the best person in the world to entrust with this task.

He searched for the emotional and logical reasons that would be most compelling to the King -- and those that would likely lead to a "Yes"

Finally, the day approached and he made his presentation.
He didn't know it at the time, but the history of the world would depend on the outcome of the meeting. The King and Queen of Spain were reluctant to agree at first, but as the presentation went on they became increasingly interested and persuaded.

The King was most impressed by Columbus's passion, his conviction and the quality of his preparation. As a result, Columbus persuaded King Ferdinand and Queen Isabella of Spain to fund an expedition with 90 crew and three ships.

No one (including the King) expected him to succeed.

On August 2nd 1492 his voyage began. It lasted 71 days. Through the voyage and return trip, Columbus and his crew had to endure near starvation, threatening storms, immense waves and a near rebellion from the crew.

Finally, on October 12th 1494 Columbus landed on an island near Florida.

A New world was discovered.
Many voyages followed the first one.

We owe Columbus, one of the greatest salespeople in history, a debt of gratitude for his hard work, his determination and his willingness to take a calculated risk.

- He had a mission he believed in.
- He successfully marketed and positioned himself with the King of Spain as the man that was the most qualified, experienced and talented to get the job done.
- He mapped out a detailed plan to reach his destination.
- He was able to take action and motivate himself and others to achieve their goals
- He overcame adversity, rejection and frustration during his journey.
- His voyage was successful and he discovered the 'new world"

In short, he stacked the odds in his favor and he closed the sale. The rest, as they say, is history.

* * *

Fast forward to the present day.

When you look at successful people and companies, it's often easy to believe and to explain away their success as primarily due to the fact that they had access to more money, more talent and more expertise than the competition. In reality, that's simply not true. There are millions of companies and people with lots of financial resources, talent and expertise. Many of them do not achieve their goals even though they would seem to have all of the tools, advantages and resources necessary for success. Look at Apple Computer for example. Lots of companies have been selling computers for the last decade or two and many did a much better job at it than Apple did. A little more than a decade ago Apple's stock price was in the low double digits, they had a 2-3% market share and virtually no money in the bank. They were struggling to survive. Today their stock price is nearing one thousand dollars per share, Apple products have a 60% market share (in I-pads, I-phones and computers) and they have over $100 Billion in cash in the bank (and growing)

So the question is, what is the common denominator of success whether it's Steve Jobs or Christopher Columbus? When you look back at history and up to the present day, what are the critical elements or methods of thinking that can help achieve personal and professional success?

I believe there are three things that top businesses; top entrepreneurs and top salespeople do better than everyone else that accounts for the majority of their success. These three things have to do with a particular mindset, a pattern, a belief, and a way of approaching the world differently than everyone else. If you don't get anything else out of all of the ideas in this book, just take away this one idea and use it. This idea is literally one of the world's most simple yet powerful ideas

The three things you need to focus on to be a great salesperson, leader or innovator are:

1. Why? Why do people and companies do the things they do?
2. How? How do they do it? How do they offer a unique advantage to the marketplace?
3. What? What do they actually sell to their customers?

Almost everyone out there in the world knows what he or she actually sells and what he or she does on a day-to-day basis. Just ask anyone what they do and you will hear statements like: I am a financial advisor. I am a banker. I am an IT Engineer. Most people also know how they do it. They are used to repeating a certain habit or pattern of doing business each day. But the vast majority of people do not know **WHY** they do what they do. This is a critically important distinction.

Most people when asked say that they do what they do to earn money or earn a paycheck. While it's true that we all need to pay our bills, money should not be the end result. It is a side benefit, a result, a by-product of what happens when you sell something, but it should not be the driving reason or purpose for what we do. For many people pursuit of money is a valid answer for them and it explains to a great degree why they are not truly as successful as they could be at what they do every day. These people often focus from the outside in, on #3 the products or what they sell first, then #2 how they sell it and most never think about #1 or their internal motivation or why they do what they do.

The real leaders, the real innovators act from the inside out. They focus on the "Why?" question first. They realize that unless they can find a compelling why reason to get up and excited about what they do each day the what and how matter a lot less. People who can answer this why question first are focused on a cause that is bigger than themselves, an over-riding purpose, a belief that guides and concentrates all their actions. Steve Jobs and Apple, Christopher Columbus and every other person that has made an impact on the world has always focused on why first, then how and finally what. Steve Jobs and Apple were and are all about "thinking differently" than everyone else. Think about it. Apple had access to the very same talent, same consultants, same engineers and same resources as their competitors in Silicon Valley.

Apple, however, focused on changing the world by first thinking *differently* and making products that were different that everyone else at the time. Products that to this day are elegantly designed, attractive and easy to use. People buy Apple products because they make their lives easier; they look good and are fun and easy to use. Most other competitors failed miserably in competing with Apple in the categories of attractive, fun and easy to use.

Steve Jobs once said in an interview that he only hired people that were passionate about what they did and used to disappointment and failure. The reason for this is because he wanted people to work for him that were truly passionate about and fully believed in what Apple was all about. People that were comfortable taking risks. He knew that there would be many long nights, frustration, failures and setbacks along the way and that if people were coming to work just for a paycheck that they would never have the drive and motivation to persevere and succeed. If they could not answer the why question he would not hire them.

Columbus thought the same way. He wanted to discover the new world. That was the why. He was passionate and he believed in what he was doing. Then he focused on how he would do it and what the result would be. Again, the sequence here is what's important. If you can create a compelling reason or find the "why" in what you do every day, if you can motivate yourself and focus your talents and energy, this can serve as your guide and compass that will keep you excited, motivated and passionate about who you are and what you do each day. Selling investments is not all that exciting or all that fun. Neither is selling computers.

Helping people achieve their lifelong retirement dreams and improving the lives of yourself, your family and many others in the process IS a compelling why.

* * *

Imagine a top salesperson is competing for a deal that could help him meet and exceed his annual sales goals by 150%. He believes 100% in his skills, capabilities and products and is on a mission to be the top salesperson in the company. He has held several preliminary meetings with his contacts at the firm and he is going to pick up one of the executives and take him out to a quick lunch and an afternoon of golf. If he makes this sale, he could earn more income than most people earn in an entire year. That's important to him, of course, but even more importantly; if he wins the deal he will be a hero to his regional manager and stand out among his peers and competitors. He might even put a deposit on that vacation home that he has wanted for years.

As he walks into the meeting to pick up the executive for lunch and golf, he is suddenly and unexpectedly directed into a large conference room filled with people. Before he goes to lunch, his contact asks him to quickly present some of his ideas and recommendations to the team of executives before him. It turns out that since everyone is in town today, they wanted to take this opportunity to hear from him personally. His casual lunch meeting with one person has suddenly turned into a group meeting with a team of high-powered executives.

First impressions matter. The stakes are high and it's time to perform.

He smiles as he steps up to the whiteboard at the front of the conference room. He is confident that he will do well. He will rely on his background, training and experience to pull him through this tight spot --and hopefully, he will make a positive impression and win the deal.

* * *

Thirty thousand feet above a lonely stretch of hot Nevada desert, a war game is taking place. A voice crackles over the radio from the ground radar site and advises the pilot that three unidentified targets are approaching him from the east. The targets do not have friendly transponders and they are approaching at over 700 miles per hour. "These are not civilian aircraft" the radar site advises the pilot. Within seconds, the altitude of these targets begins to drop rapidly and they appear to be taking a series of threatening actions.

Immediately, the pilot's training and experience kicks in. Without hesitation, he reaches out and hits the afterburners, instantly dumping dozens of gallons of fuel into the engine. A tongue of flame shoots out of the engines as he is slammed back into his seat. The plane quickly accelerates to intercept the targets as the pilot's G-suit expands to prevent him from passing out due to the increased force of gravity. He takes a deep breath as his weight increases to nearly six times his normal weight.

Next, the pilot pushes the stick over and begins a dive towards the ground as he quickly loses altitude. The airframe of his aircraft creaks and groans from the increased stress due to the speed and pressure. As he dives towards the ground, without any conscious thought the pilot engages his countermeasures and attempts to get a missile lock on the three rapidly approaching enemy targets. He is ready for a fight and he is ready to win. He has been in this situation before and has trained extensively for it. Now it's game time.

WHAT IS THE COMMON DENOMINATOR BETWEEN EACH OF THESE DIVERSE EXPERIENCES?

In each situation, there are very high stakes. Money. Power. Careers on the line and even in some cases the balance between life and death. The environment in each situation is filled with intense psychological pressure, uncertainty and stress.

What will allow each of these diverse these professionals to perform at the highest levels and maximize their chances of success whether it is on an important sales call or in a $30 million dollar aircraft?

As we have just learned, there are *several main factors* that will determine the success or failure of each of the individuals mentioned above. In a moment, we will learn what these factors are and we will apply them to a very specific area of opportunity in the financial services business. Throughout the rest of this book, we will discover how to apply each of these four factors successfully in your investment and financial planning practice.

Although these techniques and strategies we will discuss can be used successfully for any type of sales, I'll focus much of our discussion in this book on using these concepts and applying them to the financial services business- and in particular the retirement income-planning marketplace.

The reason for this is simple.

This market is booming and it will remain the #1 opportunity in the financial services business for the next decade or more. It is an area that you should be not only aware of but also passionate about if you are serious about the financial services business.

If you catch this wave and can capitalize on it the right way by becoming an expert and specialist, you will be able to rapidly boost your income and build your business in a way that might seem almost unimaginable just a few years ago.

If you miss this wave, however, and continue to business "the old way" by staying a generalist in the business, the coming years are likely to be very frustrating, financially challenging and for many advisors, potentially fatal to their business.

Now how can I say this? This is a very big claim to make.

Here's why.

In the military there is a phrase that says to win a war one needs to win the 'hearts and minds' of the people. This can't be done by dropping more bombs on them- it can only be done by helping them see the long-term value that you are bringing to their society. It needs to be seen and experienced by the local population as they see roads being built, schools being built, hospitals being repaired and power plants and other parts of their infrastructure coming back to life.

In sales, you win the 'hearts and minds' of your clients and prospects by helping them ***solve specific problems and challenges*** they have and by building relationships with them over time.

What, you might ask, is one of the best ways you can build relationships with qualified clients and prospects? By providing them with simple and effective solutions that meet their most pressing financial needs.

What, you might ask, is one of the biggest financial needs that every one of the clients and prospects that you speak with have?

Everyone needs to have a written detailed retirement income plan to help him or her attain and live the lifestyle they desire at retirement.

While retirement planning may be complex, the plan you develop for clients can and should be very simple- even as short as 2-3 pages. Recent studies by industry experts have shown that between 5-15% of Americans have a written detailed retirement income plan that has been developed and implemented by a financial professional.

This leaves the vast majority of the American public without a plan, without a roadmap for retirement and as a result, very little chance of experiencing a "successful retirement"

You can change this. This can be your reason why you do what you do each day.

So ask yourself, what business are you and I really in? What is our true objective for our business? What do we want to accomplish over the long term?

The truth is, that at the most basic level, we are in the business of gathering assets under management by acquiring new clients. Once we have these assets under management we either charge a fee for our services or we invest clients in commissionable products and services that provide revenue to our practice. The more qualified clients and prospects we interact with on an ongoing basis, the more clients we will acquire and the more money we will make.

Sounds simple enough, right?

Then why do so many advisors worry so much about prospecting and growing their business? Why are we kept up at night worrying about losing big accounts to the competition and wondering if our income will go up or down dramatically from year to year?

I would propose that one of the key reasons for these challenges that we all face is that we have not clearly defined up front what the true "mission" of our business is.

It's a fact that as advisors we are selling commodity products and services. When you or I sell or buy a commodity (like oil, gasoline, coffee or corn for example), in the absence of any way to differentiate the product, people always look for a lower price and a better service when deciding where to place their order. All things being equal, if people can get your product somewhere else quickly and for less, they will often move their business to the competition. Unless, of course, in advance you have built up the perceived value of your product or services so that people decide that it's too much of a headache or too much of a problem to switch.

That's what successful branding is all about isn't it? - Getting people to have a positive experience with your company and to believe that the quality product or service you offer provides value that exceeds the cost. Once you have established this belief, customers won't need to think a lot about buying from you in the future. They know what to expect and they will just 'do it.' A good part of successful marketing revolves around how customers perceive your product or service.

Take a commodity like water for example. This is something that we get for free shipped right into our homes through ordinary pipes. Pepsi, the company that owns Aquafina water sells tens of millions of bottles of water each year. This water is <u>not</u> spring water; in fact, it's the same type of municipal water that you and I can get right out of the faucet.

In fact, Pepsi had to acknowledge this fact publicly in July of 2007 (see below)

"NEW YORK (Reuters) -- PepsiCo Inc. will spell out that its Aquafina bottled water is made with tap water, a concession to the growing environmental and political opposition to the bottled water industry."

Now why in the world would someone pay $3.99 for a 6 pack of water when they could get the same thing for free right in their house? Why do people buy an estimated 9 billion gallons of this bottled water annually?

Here is the secret.
This has direct application to your business.
It can grow your practice- and your revenue stream if applied correctly.

It doesn't require tens of thousands of dollars in advertising.

Good marketing and effective branding create demand by creating and reinforcing the perception that in this case, the bottled water is somehow better and safer for you if it is bottled vs. consumed out of the tap. Notice that the product and the quality is exactly the same, but the price is different due to the perceived value. The customer has learned (and been trained through advertising) to believe that bottled water is cleaner and has a better taste- even though it is exactly the same as the water coming out of their tap.

Perception is reality.

One could argue that we need to do this same type of innovative marketing for our investment practice to differentiate ourselves and the true value we bring to the table for clients. Fortunately, we don't need to be tricky marketers; we can simply develop a way to differentiate our service from everyone else in our town.

Every advisor in your hometown can sell mutual funds, annuities, managed accounts and exchange traded funds. They all are selling the same hot funds and likely have identical sales pitches (thanks in no doubt to their regional wholesaler)

Your challenge—and mine—in the coming years is to "bullet proof" your practice in a way that keeps your best clients happy and satisfied and attracts dozens or even hundreds of additional clients to you that look just like your best, most profitable clients.

One of the best ways you can accomplish this goal is to become an expert or a specialist in a certain segment of the marketplace.

So the question is, where should you focus your limited energy and marketing dollars?

Where do your clients have the greatest need for your services?

In the retirement income-planning marketplace.

Your mission should be to dominate the retirement income marketplace in your local community in the next 12 months. You should own it to such an extent that any time someone asks one of their friends in your community who they should talk to about retirement or retirement planning that your name comes up as the answer.

So how can you do this?

Read on. That's one of the key strategies you will learn in this book.

Your ability to capitalize on this critical retirement income need that your clients and prospects have will to a great extent determine the success of your financial services practice far into the future. This is the "Why" question we discussed earlier. The reason you do what you do should be to help the tens of millions of prospects out there that need a plan for their future. By the end of this book you will be uniquely qualified to deliver on that plan.

To capitalize successfully on the opportunity, you will need to know and apply four specific concepts.

With an estimated 77 Million "baby boomers" poised to retire in the next 10-15 years, you will need to be able to:

1. ***Learn the process*** for developing a retirement income plan that is simple, easy for the average retail client to understand and requires a minimum of effort to implement across your entire client base.
2. ***Learn how to brand*** and position yourself and your practice as having retirement income planning expertise.
3. ***Learn how to effectively communicate with***, ***market to and present yourself to*** clients and prospects in your community in a way that makes them **WANT TO** do business with you.
4. ***Learn how to effectively target, engage and motivate*** the right customers and prospects that need the expertise and advice that you are offering.

Obviously, doing these four things well with each of your clients and prospects is something that won't happen overnight or by luck or accident.

It's something that you have to decide to do -- and it's something that you need to invest the time and energy in if you want to become successful at it.

This leads into the second key theme of the book.

Before you get to the phase of winning the bigger war and driving dozens or even hundreds of new investment clients into your retirement income business, you first need to understand the current battlefield in which you are fighting and look for areas to exploit.

The majority of your competition is fighting the war with the same old products and the same old ideas.

In this environment, it's ***almost impossible*** to differentiate yourself sufficiently in the minds of your prospects.

During the revolutionary war, entire armies lined up in straight lines to face each other at close quarters. Then, seemingly at the agreed upon time, they attacked each other according to the rigid rules of war.

Hundreds of thousands of people died.

In later years, this method of warfare changed dramatically with the invention of the machine gun. Then it evolved again with the invention of the tank, artillery and use of aircraft in battle. Now it has evolved again with advanced body armor, direct energy weapons and unmanned aerial vehicles.

Those that continued to fight according to the old rules were systematically wiped out. The same is true in sales. If you don't evolve and learn, you die.

But your not one of those people. You have a secret weapon.

By learning and applying basic retirement income planning concepts with your clients and prospects you can differentiate yourself from your competition.

The information, technology and strategies you gain in the coming pages will enable you to dominate the battlefield.

You will then be able to almost effortlessly gain ground and take territory (and sales) away from your competition.

How can you do this? You need to have to have the right type of training delivered to you so that you can run each of your new prospects and clients through a specific process or system for developing a written retirement income plan.

There are specific rules and principals that you need to follow in order to help your clients develop a written income plan.

The plans you develop should be designed to provide clients with the predictable income and the growth that they need so that their income will last throughout their lifetime. We'll learn more about this later on.

Throughout this book, we are going to be looking at the sales process that top sales people go through and compare it metaphorically against the process that the U.S. Navy's TOP GUN pilots go through in their training at the Fallon Naval Air Station in Fallon, Nevada, U.S.A.

The reason for this is simple. The pilots that get accepted into the TOP GUN program are among the best in the Navy.

Even though they are among the best pilots that the Navy has, the job of TOP GUN training is to give them the winners edge and make them *even better* at what they do.

The mental and physical preparation combined with the academic learning and hands on combat training that these pilots go through in TOP GUN is in a sense very similar to the mental and physical stress that you and I as salespeople are subjected to each and every day in the business world.

Instead of a fighter jet, we drive a car.

Instead of pulling "G" forces in a turn, we spend long days and sometimes nights out meeting prospects and customers.

Instead of dropping bombs and explosives, we "drop" tickets, enroll people and close sales orders.

THE NATURAL LAWS OF SELLING

There are *natural laws* that govern the sales process much like the *natural laws* that govern aerodynamics. An aircraft's wingspan, the shape of the wing and the speed of the air flowing over the wings create lift and drag and allow the aircraft to become airborne. The *natural laws of selling*, which *include clearly identifying your target market, creating a compelling value proposition to your target audience, building rapport, utilizing demographic and psychographic profiling, applying the magic of fact-finding, sales scripting and story selling and creating endless referrals from your book of satisfied clients*- will all play a key role in governing your future sales success.

These skills will help determine the final altitude you reach in your sales career.

Without a firm understanding of these laws and how they can positively impact your business and sales effectiveness, you may never get off the ground.

You and I both know that selling is primarily a mental game, not a physical one -and that mental game is often fought out every day in that space between your ears.

Getting up early day after day, picking up the phone and making or taking numerous calls and staying motivated, positive and upbeat -despite the constant challenges that clients and prospects can throw at you can be difficult and sometimes discouraging.

But you push through this anyway and move onward.

The same is true with precision flying. Physical skill gets you into the cockpit of the aircraft, but your mental skill- your focus; your discipline; your control over your emotions- and your skills of effective decision making under pressure make all the difference between success and failure up in the sky.

The same is true in selling.

If there were any justice in the world, we would have all learned how to develop our powers of focus, our persuasion skills and a passion for what we do in our formal schooling.

But the fact is, most of us were never taught how to do this.

There is no University that you can enroll in to develop the 'mental mindset' of a top performer or to become a retirement income-planning expert.

There is no single course that you can take that will teach you about communication, influence, branding and how to apply the power of personal marketing on your behalf.

There is, however, this book.

THE TOP GUN FIGHTER WEAPONS SCHOOL

In 1968, American Air Force and Navy pilots found themselves in an unusual and unfamiliar predicament.

They were losing the Air war over North Vietnam.

The kill ratio of enemy fighters shot down to U.S. planes shot down was a shocking 2:1. For every two enemy fighters shot down, one American plane would be shot down. How could this possibly happen? The U.S. had clear technological superiority and was fighting against a society that was technologically backward. *So how were the U.S. Pilots getting beaten so badly?*

In the business world, this was like having a company that produces the *best quality product*, that incorporates the *latest and best technology*, that supports it's products with one of the *largest marketing budgets* and sales teams in the industry - and it still gets 'trampled' by the competition.

How could a small competitor with less skill, fewer resources and inferior technology beat a strong established company like this?

It happens all of the time in business.

It has happened in the past to big well-established companies like Xerox, Coca-Cola, IBM, Nokia, RIMM, Proctor and Gamble (and many others, past and present) That's why it's a fallacy to blame any 'sales slumps' you or I might have exclusively on the marketing team, the service people or the product development people.

It's not really about the product anyway. The "best" most sophisticated products rarely win in the marketplace.

The winners are the products and services that are *targeted precisely, positioned creatively and marketed wisely*. You need all three elements working in tandem to win the war.

In your role as a professional salesperson, you are at the 'tip of the spear' -meeting with prospects every day. You know what is REALLY going on - and how prospects actually react in the real world. You know, much like the TOP GUN instructors, that it's often *the training, the skill, the agility and the talent* of the individual pilot flying the plane that makes all the difference- *not the plane itself.*

The History Of Top Gun

Back in the Pentagon during the 1960's, the Military brass had become enamored with new technology (i.e. new 'products') and the value of standoff attack missiles. The military experts of the day believed that U.S. aircrews would not even have to see the enemy to knock them out of the sky. They could simply shoot a missile at them from dozens of miles away while remaining safely out of reach of an enemy's guns and weapons.

This was the theory of the day, and it was being proved *wrong* each and every day in actual practice over the skies of North Vietnam. The planners in the Pentagon and the aviators out at sea had forgotten and neglected one of the most basic and important skills of air warfare. The importance of Air Combat Maneuvering (ACM) or "Dog-Fighting."

This focus by the Pentagon on new technology is very much like the explosion of current product innovations taking place today in the mutual fund and insurance business around retirement income planning. The introduction of "living benefits" in the variable annuity world and the development of new types of mutual funds and managed accounts that are designed to provide both sustainable income and growth are being positioned and marketed as the "magic bullets" to help solve all of your clients retirement income planning needs.

Although many of these products do offer some value and they meet a key client need (typically safety of principal and a predictable rate of growth or income) the problem is that the average retail clients are looking for *simple easy to understand solutions.*

Anyone who has actually read a variable annuity prospectus that describes how living benefits actually work has no doubt quickly realized that many of these products are not simple, easy to understand solutions.

In fact, living benefits are getting more and more complicated as companies try to gain additional market share by coming out with even more features and benefits.

Products are part of the solution, but not THE solution. The winners of this battle will not necessarily be those that build a better mousetrap (because someone else will always quickly develop a new living benefit or lower cost mutual fund or managed account solution that will be quickly copied by a competitor), but rather, the benefits will accrue to those firms and those advisors that become *specialists at retirement income planning* and those that can *explain and successfully deliver* a retirement income plan solution to clients in a simple and easy to understand fashion.

First you need to understand the process and be able to explain it to the client, AND THEN you present the appropriate product solutions as part of the income plan.

YOUR MOST IMPORTANT SELLING RESOURCE

I've spent the much of the past two-decades studying what sets top performers apart. From 1989 to 1996, along with my brother Mark Magnacca, I built my own successful independent financial advisory business in the Boston area, called Wellesley Financial Services, Inc. I grew my business primarily through presenting financial education seminars to corporations, associations, and non- profit institutions.

As a result of my early success in the investment business, I also co-founded and ran a successful sales training business called Peak Performance Development Inc.

In the investment world, I began my career in the independent broker-dealer channel, where there was very limited training and support. The truth is that *most* sales training that people receive isn't sales *training* at all. At many companies, training often centers on 'product training' and typically overlooks the importance of interpersonal communication, rapport building, ethical influence and the need for good fact-finding as part of the sales process.

This is like training a pilot to drop bombs and shoot missiles BEFORE training him on the basics of flying. Both skills are necessary, but the sequence of the training makes all the difference.

Individuals and firms cannot dominate every market that is available, but they can dominate a specific market.

The market that you choose to dominate should be growing rapidly now and in the future.

It should encompass your most profitable clients.

It should be large enough so that your pool of prospects to contact numbers in the hundreds or thousands in your geographic area.

The retirement income market fits <u>all</u> of these criteria.

WHAT WARREN BUFFETT THINKS
ABOUT RETIREMENT INCOME

It may help you to think about the retirement income-planning marketplace as an investment opportunity. Evaluate it the way you would evaluate any other potential opportunity. This can be a huge opportunity for your business, but should you invest your valuable time and energy in it to become an expert?

Warren Buffett, the world's most successful investor looks for investment opportunities that are:

1. **Simple** to understand
2. Provide a **sustainable competitive advantage**
3. Have **above average economic returns and profit potential**

Think about the retirement income-planning marketplace for a moment. It is simple to understand at its most basic level. Approximately 77 Million investors will need a written retirement income plan and about 85-90% of these folks don't have a plan right now. You can help them create a plan and then implement that plan with the investment solutions that you sell. What typical questions do you want to answer when you develop an income plan for a client? If you can help them answer three simple questions you can easily develop a plan for them. The questions your customers and prospects want answered are:

1. *Will my income plan balance predictability of income, safety and growth?(a good plan should have elements of all three)*
2. *How much retirement money will I have at my planned retirement date under average market conditions?*
3. *How much in annual income will I be able to generate at*

retirement and each year thereafter from any pensions, social security, annuities and retirement investments (noted in #2 above)?

You can answer these key questions with a white pad and a pen, with a calculator or with a sophisticated computer simulation. The better the tool you use the more accurate and precise the result you will get. That said, 95% of people don't have a plan at all, so the white pad or calculator approach can provide significant value if you don't have access to computer simulations or planning programs.

It's as simple as that. Just answer three basic questions for clients and you can win their retirement income planning business.

You can't do retirement income planning by trying to sell clients or prospects the products first. That's what everyone else is doing and *you need to be different.* You need to be consultative and develop a simple plan that answers the three questions above. Developing the plan allows you to demonstrate your skill and expertise to the prospect. It helps you build the personal relationship and creates trust and rapport. *Then you sell the products needed to implement the plan.*

So now lets revisit Warren Buffett's philosophy on investments and how it relates to retirement income. Can you gain a ***sustainable competitive advantage*** by training yourself in income planning concepts and by positioning yourself as a retirement income-planning expert in your local community? Of course you can.

Your sustainable competitive advantage is your expertise, your training and your ability to deliver a repeatable process to your clients.

Will income planning easily produce **above average economic returns** for you and your business? You bet. It's a fact that the multiple products you will sell as a result of developing a personalized income plan or the fee your charge to develop the plan should compensate you very well for the work you do.

Typically, clients that do income planning have *greater assets and higher account balances* than any other demographic group. These clients are *motivated* to make a decision. If you do planning the right way they will consolidate and bring more assets into your firm, they will buy more mutual funds and managed accounts from you and they will buy many more annuities—all without any objections since these products are "part of the plan."

In addition, when you do retirement income planning well, you will have an endless supply of qualified referrals from your current client base.

If you have read this far, hopefully you are convinced regarding the opportunity in the retirement income market and how it can transform your financial business.

In the coming chapters I will show you how to use the latest selling skills and persuasion techniques to position yourself as a retirement income expert, communicate your value proposition to prospective clients and generate more income for yourself and your business with less time and effort.

Lets take the next step.

CHAPTER 1
Developing The TOP GUN Mindset

"A fighter pilot has to be incredibly devoted and passionate about being the best. Every time you go up on a combat mission or training mission you goal is to win every time. There are no points for second best."

TOP GUN Pilot
Call Sign "Rattler"

What's ahead in this chapter:
Before we start positioning you as a retirement income-planning expert, I want to spend a bit of time in this chapter helping you understand the top gun mindset. You need to understand how virtually all successful people get themselves to easily make changes in their personal and professional lives. While becoming an expert at retirement income planning is not all that difficult, it will require that you change the way you think about your business. During the learning process you may start to ask yourself questions like "Well, my business is different and that may not work" or "This is a bit different than what I am used to, should I risk my client relationships by trying these ideas out?" These questions are common ones- and if you don't develop the right mindset in advance, they will serve to immediately demotivate you and prevent you from applying the ideas in this book. I don't want that to happen, so I want you to better understand how most successful people are able to quickly change

1

their beliefs, attitudes and mental mindset in a way that supports them in achieving their goals.

When you look at our society and witness individuals performing at high levels of performance- whether it be in sports, athletics, business, sales or entertainment, It's easy to believe that these high performing individuals are all especially gifted, talented or lucky (or a combination of all three)

The 'secret' to success, however, has less to do with raw talent or luck and much more to do with having a belief and a passion for what you do every day. What I've found by studying top performers is that although there is no shortcut to success, success can be created by combining the key elements of passion, strategy and then taking action. This chapter will show you how to develop and maintain the passion to win.

By adopting the beliefs of excellence and becoming truly passionate about what you do, you will be able to break through the mental barriers that may have held you back in the past. Breaking these barriers will be the first step in your journey to transform your business, your sales career--and ultimately your life.

DEVELOPING YOUR PASSION TO WIN

PASSION. It's an emotionally loaded word. Is this something that some people just innately possess and others simply do not? Or is it something that can be acquired, nurtured and grown by anyone with the right desire and skills? The answer, of course, is that passion is available to all of us – at any time. The key is unlocking it.

Beliefs and passion are two emotional states that are closely linked together for most high achievers. You can be very passionate about something but still not achieve your goal and objective <u>unless</u> you believe your goal is possible and attainable. One the other hand, you can believe you can accomplish a goal but unless you're passionate about it and relentlessly pursue it, chances are you will get disappointed by the speed-bumps that life throws at you and will not get the result you want. Think of all of the frustration that Steve Jobs and his staff went through as they developed the I-phone and I-pad. Without their passion to persevere, despite the challenges they faced, the world would be a very different place today. Both of these emotions PASSION AND BELIEFS need to be pulling in the same direction.

You might be wondering, how does a fighter pilot become passionate about what he or she does every day? Some might perceive that the job of a fighter pilot could be extremely dangerous, detail orientated and complex. On a daily basis, the "job" involves complete mastery of a wide variety of complex disciplines including aeronautics, engineering, meteorology and advanced weapons systems and tactics just to name a few. It seems like a lot of work just to have the opportunity (all too infrequently in some cases) to conduct flight operations. Most pilots put in a considerable amount of training time compared to the actual flight time that they conduct. Often, pilots spend up to 10 hours of training for every 1 hour of actual flight time. This is often necessary because they are dealing with life and death situations. The split second decisions that each pilot makes—or fails to make—could be the difference between life and death in the sky.

In part, it is this challenge and this high level of risk that is created from dealing with an unpredictable situation that often creates the excitement, passion and adrenaline rush that most fighter pilots are looking for. Often, one could say much the same about most successful salespeople. They often dislike the paperwork that they have to do, the 'cold calling' the sales skill training and all of the preparation work that needs to be done prior to and sometimes after the sale—but they do it so they can experience the thrill, the excitement and the adrenaline rush of closing a big deal or making a big sale. If this is true, (and it is) it provides us with a clue regarding how to develop the passion to win and how to develop the beliefs and attitudes of a TOP GUN sales performer.

THE TOP GUN MINDSET

Have you every wondered how two similar people from similar backgrounds and similar personal histories can react completely differently when confronted with the same external event? How is it that one salesperson can lose a big sale and decide that this means that they are not 'cut out' for the business and need to do something else - while another salesperson confronted with the same experience of losing a big sale will use this experience to pick himself up, refocus his energies and continue to drive forward with renewed enthusiasm and vigor?

What's the difference between the good pilots who "wash out" of advanced combat training and those that 'stick it out?' What is the difference between each class of recruits in the Navy SEAL training that 'make it' and the vast majority of others that decide that they can't take it anymore, ring the 'drop on request' bell and drop out of the class and leave the training altogether?

Each person is exposed to exactly the same training, but there is a radical difference in who makes it and who does not. Often, the difference is a mental one, not a physical one.

What is it that motivates these professionals to endure all the training, intense hardships and physical and mental exhaustion? What is it that motivates them to work the long hours for little pay? What is it that causes them to put their life on the line day after day? *A belief that what they are doing is important and a passion to be the best.*

So, what is the difference, the mental edge that causes one person to persevere and another to fail? And if there is a secret to this success and it can be learned and replicated (and it can) how *can we learn and apply this mental mindset to create the winners edge in our sale careers?*

Let's take a moment to explore one important facet of the military's training process and learn how they *mentally condition* elite troops for success. Part of this training involves helping the recruits rapidly *change the beliefs and associations* or the 'bar codes' they have around their own personal limits and their capabilities in a way that helps them adopt a 'can do' attitude. I'll share this concept with you in a story.

'PROGRAMMING' YOURSELF FOR SUCCESS

A short drive away from my house is a "Six Flags" amusement park. Last summer I took my family to Six Flags for a family outing. I have three young sons and for those of you that have children of any age you know that an amusement park has an almost irresistible, magnetic pull on both young kids and older adults. Part of the reason for the appeal is that an amusement park can be a special place to feel more alive by having fun testing one's limits in a relatively safe environment.

I remember watching my son and a friend of his who is the same age getting ready to take their first roller coaster ride. They were excited and smiling in the line waiting for the roller coaster. I was going to go on the ride with them and sit in the seat right behind them. The day before our trip, my son and I had talked at length about what the experience in the roller coaster would be like. He was a bit nervous and not sure he wanted to go on the roller coaster. We discussed the speed that the cars would be traveling at, we anticipated the sound of the kids screaming in excitement, we talked about what the shake and rattle of the roller coaster cars would feel like. We even got the chance to watch a show on roller coasters on the Discovery Channel the day before we went to the park. The kids on the Discovery show were having a great time riding a wide variety of roller coasters. They were excited, smiling and screaming with joy and anticipation.

A number of years ago, I remembered reading a psychological study about treating children to overcome phobias and fears. The study concerned children that were afraid of dogs. The way the researchers would treat the children was not with weeks of expensive therapy or frequent medication, but surprisingly, they treated them by letting them watch a short 15-minute videotape. Interestingly, the researchers had found that when they showed children *a videotape* of children their own age laughing and having a good time and petting and playing with a dog then when children were confronted with a *real dog* **over 85%** of the children were able to approach and pet a real dog without any fear. That's a big deal. Going from an intense phobia of dogs to petting them and interacting with them after a 15-minute video.

Later on in the book we're going to learn a bit more about a concept of *social proof.* This powerful unconscious tool basically states that *when human beings are confronted with an unfamiliar situation- and they are not sure how to react and respond- they take cues and clues from other people around them to help guide them regarding the best way to react and behave.*

Make a 'mental note' of this concept- it's one of the most powerful and often-overlooked tools of influence that you have available to you in your sales toolbox.

The show that my son watched with me the day before our trip to the amusement park was a form of 'social proof' that communicated the message that roller coasters are safe, fun and exciting.

Here is the interesting thing.

On our first roller-coaster ride my son was smiling and shouting and having a great time. His friend next to him who had not had the benefit of my pep talk in advance of the ride- or watching the roller coaster videotape- started screaming. He was screaming not in excitement, but in sheer terror. It seemed that my son's friends initial confidence evaporated quickly once the ride began to move.

This was not a good situation to be in, especially with someone else's child. Although I could not stop the ride, I tried to calm this boy down as best I could. Fortunately, the ride was only two minutes long.

But it was a *long* two minutes. As we pulled into the station, I tried to console and help my son's friend the best I could, but he was a blubbering mess. I felt terrible that I let him go on the ride and wondered if I had just played a role in creating a lifelong fear of roller coasters in this child (Fortunately, as it turns out, I didn't.)

My son, of course, immediately asked to do the ride again. His friend, on the other hand, excused himself to the restroom to recover from his ordeal.

To this day though, my son's friend really isn't that interested in roller coasters.

The experience got me thinking. Imagine two adult people sitting side by side in the front row of a roller coaster ride. Both of them are going to experience *exactly the same* physical experiences on the ride. The rush of wind through their hair, the noise of the screaming passengers, the feeling of the car moving and rattling down the tracks, the sight of the landscape and park out in front of them. The pounding of their heart. The same exact physical sensations take place, but one of the passengers can label, interpret or barcode his experience as "I feel sick let me off this thing" while a person in the seat right next to him can be having a great time and say "I love this..it's awesome".

The exact same inputs happen, but two radically different experiences or outcomes result. The reality is that it's not what happens to you that makes the difference, it's what you decide to do with what happens that decides your future.

Often, we look to external events that happen on our lives and believe that these *external events* that happen to us control how we feel, what we think and how we should behave. The *reality is* that it's not the external events that happen in our lives that determine how we should feel, it's the *meaning* that we choose or decide to 'link' to or associate to these events that shapes our feelings and behaviors.

Meaning and associations are something we learn.

During Navy SEAL training, for example, the teams of recruits are trained to actually enjoy repeatedly lifting a 300 pound log over their heads in order to demonstrate commitment and teamwork. In contrast, one of the 'punishment' logs the instructors make the recruits use weighs 600+ pounds and is named, appropriately, "Old Misery." Over time, the recruits are *trained* to *associate* a degree of pleasure with the intense physical conditioning they endure as part of their training because they know that if they make it through, then they will be part of a very exclusive group. They are passionate about being the best they can be and they start learning that the harder they work in training the better prepared they will be in real life combat.

The fact is that people can learn and be trained to associate both pain and pleasure to a wide variety of stimuli.

Think of the process this way. A good metaphor to use is to think of the mind as an exceptionally efficient computer. Attached to the computer is a bar code scanner. When something goes past the scanner, it reads the bar code and automatically knows what the product is and what price to charge. In much the same way, human beings automatically attach bar codes or labels to experiences that they have throughout their lifetime and these bar codes tell your brain *how to feel* about any experience and *how you should respond*. This system of coding memories has enabled human beings to survive, learn and prosper for thousands of years. The problem is, no one has ever told us how to control or interrupt this 'coding' process if it's not working to support us in achieving our goals- it just happens automatically outside of our conscious awareness.

Here is the real interesting thing. Just like changing the price on an item at the store can be done either by changing the computer program in the back office or by changing the bar code attached to the item, *anyone* has the ability to change the bar code on any experience that they have had in the past or the present. Like many things in life, it's easy- if you know how to do it.

Using The Fear Factor To Your Advantage

Don't take my word for it however. Consider the following. One of NBC's most highly rated and successful "reality" shows of recent years is a show called *Fear Factor*. If you haven't seen it you haven't missed a real lot from an intellectual point of view. That being said, much like rubbernecking on the highway as you pass a car accident, Fear Factor often compels you to watch even though you know better. On the show they always have very good-looking young men and woman performing a wide variety of physical and mental tasks. The goal of the show is to watch as these contestants subject themselves to eating things like sheep eyes, Madagascar spitting cockroaches, tarantulas and cow intestines just to name a few examples. The more disgusting the feat, the better viewers like it!

Now why am I sharing this with you? For most of us, the thought of eating a giant helping of sheep eyes or live tarantulas would not only be disgusting and repulsive, but we would "never", ever do it.

Here is the interesting thing. What if you are the type of person that, like many people, works hard each day and likes money because of the wonderful things that you can buy with it?

What if you were offered the potential to win $50,000 and have the opportunity to be seen by millions of viewers across the United States? Some of us would still say, "No way, I still would not do it." For other people this would be a huge motivator and they would go ahead. It all depends on your beliefs and personal values. We'll discuss this a bit more later on in the book when we explore the concept of 'values' and psychographic profiling in greater detail.

Fear Factor has hundreds of otherwise sane people trying desperately for a chance to eat all sorts of disgusting stuff and perform all sorts of stunts for just the chance to win $50,000 on the show. What's the point here?

Let's suppose you were offered $100,000 or even $1,000,000 to eat a bowl of sheep eyes. Would you do it? As the dollar amounts increase, chances are you would begin to *re-evaluate* what you would and would not do. You might begin to change your associations and ask yourself questions like "I know that eating sheep eyes is disgusting and painful in the short run, but if I actually suffer for just a few minutes and I do it and win, I sure could do a lot of amazing, pleasurable things with all the money." What if someone had a gun to your head - or to the head of someone you loved? Would you do it then? **Of course you would.**

OUR PRODUCT MAY KILL YOU

Cigarettes are products that most medical experts now agree may kill you- if you use them enough over time- but tens of millions of people still buy them. Why?

Advertisers have been able to successfully link *prestige, class, success, sex, athletic achievement* and a host of other positive attributes to these products and services and as a result, people buy them.

Think about it.

If advertisers linked what *really happens* when people use Cigarettes and Alcohol products in large quantities over time, no one would buy them. Imagine advertisements showing 'the night after' a big party where people had too much to drink- with people smelling bad, vomiting all over the floor and having horrible headaches. Or think about a cigarette ad featuring a person in an intensive care ward who has emphysema and can't breathe- someone who will have to have an oxygen tank strapped to their back for the rest of their life. Not a real positive association.

That's the level of influence in our society today. If marketers can get people to think that alcohol and cigarettes are *sexy and desirable* and they are able to sell tens of *billions of dollars* of these products annually, think of how effective they can be at selling a decent product that doesn't kill you or make you feel sick.

Something to think about isn't it?

Remember, associations are *learned,* and marketing is all about *shaping perceptions* and creating *favorable associations* between your products and the things people want most in life.

So in it's most basic form, that's what the influence process is all about. Linking positive states and emotions to your product and service. This process of influence is going on all around you right now- whether or not you want to acknowledge it.

Let me give you one final example of the power of advertising and branding. Would you like to own a Mercedes Benz? If you answered yes, *why* do you want a Mercedes Benz? Think about it for a moment. The answers I typically get are things like "because it's the best and I'm the best, so I want the best." Or I might hear something like "Well, because the feeling it will give me. If I own one, then I feel that I am successful" This is purely an emotional decision, not a logical one. The reality is, more often than not, people don't buy needs. When you go to buy a Mercedes, you're not buying it because you *need* a Mercedes, no, the truth is, you WANT it and if you want it bad enough and you can find a way to afford it, it becomes a need.

Some people, however, when asked if they would like a Mercedes respond by saying "What are you stupid? What kind of idiot would spend $50,000 or $100,000 on an automobile? For one Mercedes I could buy five or ten Ford trucks. Now why would I want to buy a Mercedes? That would be stupid." But if the advertising is done well, and targeted correctly, each ad will appeal to the right people based on their demographics, lifestyle and psychographics. We'll discuss these concepts more in the coming chapters.

The point here is that associations *can and do change* - and they can change in an INSTANT with the *proper motivation and leverage*. This has a direct linkage to the sales process because typically during the early part of the sales cycle people tend to link pain with buying. They are thinking about the sheep eyes. During the sales process, a good salesperson is able to help the client link or associate pleasure (i.e. the things that the prospect wants) with buying and pain with not buying. Once the pleasure outweighs the pain in the clients mind, the sale is often made.

Later on, we'll learn how to change any negative associations your prospects might have about salespeople or your particular product or service – and you won't have to offer anyone $50,000 or put a gun to their head to do it.

Remember, what you link pain to, and what you link pleasure to, can control and direct your destiny.

What you get your prospects and customers to link pain and pleasure to can shape and direct your sales career and the impact you have on customers and prospects now and in the future.

When you meet clients and prospects, they likely have existing beliefs, feelings, thoughts and emotions that are linked to the words that you may use to describe yourself and what you do each day. If they, for example, have *negative associations* or barcodes linked to the words "insurance agent" or "investment advisor" then we need to use a better, more engaging and compelling description for what we do in order to reach people and capture their attention. We want to get the client to say "That's interesting...tell me more"

We will learn how to do this later in the book when we discuss role statements.

WHAT THE CIA AND "EXTRAORDINARY RENDITION" CAN TEACH US ABOUT SELLING

"The standard was for every hour spent interrogating, the interrogator and his team would spend four to six hours in preparation"

-"John", CIA Interrogator

Let me provide a real world example regarding how changing beliefs can lead to changed behavior. In the intelligence world and in the "war in terror" the CIA has the difficult task of prying potentially life saving information out of enemy terrorists that can save American lives without subjecting the prisoners to torture.

A press report not too long ago discussed one technique that was used successfully by the CIA to get valuable information from an Al-Qaeda prisoner without the use of torture. Here is what they did. The prisoner was sedated and was taken to a U.S. military hospital inside of a U.S. base. The prisoner was surrounded by Arabic doctors and all of the visual and audio inputs that would be present if the prisoner were actually in a Saudi Arabian hospital.

When the prisoner woke up, the Doctors spoke to him in Arabic with Saudi accents. They looked Arabic. They told him that he had been 'rescued' and brought to Saudi Arabia for treatment and that he would never be delivered to the "infidel" Americans.

They gave him local Saudi newspapers to read.

His television received only local Saudi news programs.

Other "prisoners" he talked to confirmed the fact that he was in Saudi Arabia. (They were not *actual* prisoners but CIA plants)

Based on all of these external references, He *believed* he was safe in Saudi Arabia.

In a short period of time, he let his guard down and "broke" and began talking to the "Doctors" who were in reality CIA interrogation experts. How did the CIA do this? They controlled the surroundings, they controlled how they were perceived by the prisoner (dress, language, etc) and they controlled who he spoke with (literally his "references") These are three factors that you can also control when you meet with clients and prospects.

We'll learn more about how to do this shortly.

USING THE TOOLS OF
UNCONSCIOUS INFLUENCE

A number of years ago a university professor by the name of Dr. Robert Cialdini conducted a series of remarkable studies on persuasion, influence and selling that revealed a number of secrets regarding what Cialdini called "the tools of unconscious influence."

These tools and techniques have been used successfully for years by top salespeople, law enforcement officers and intelligence agents.

The problem that Cialdini confronted early in his research was that the top salespeople and law enforcement professionals that were using these tools were often unaware of the mechanics behind HOW they did what they did. They just talked to people and in the vast majority of cases, they were able to significantly influence their behavior.

One key objective of Cialdini's study was to discover and document the actual process and the techniques that top salespeople used unconsciously (without their awareness) to get ordinary people to *automatically comply* with and follow through on the salespersons requests. This automatic compliance was achieved *without any conscious awareness* on the part of the client that they were being influenced or persuaded.

Some of the key tools of unconscious influence that Cialdidi discovered include:

1. **Authority**- If someone is perceived as an expert or in a position of perceived authority people will listen to them and automatically comply with a request (like a Doctor in a white coat, a police officer with a badge or a service member in a military uniform or even someone with an educational credential) Although we don't like it, most of us will comply with requests from "authority figures" without thinking twice because they are perceived as experts. This is one of the reasons why becoming a retirement income planning authority and expert is so important. As an expert in this area, you will command authority and credibility with your clients and prospects. You can quickly become an authority in an area easily by gaining training, education,

credentials, publishing articles or books or simply having a well designed website. Perception is reality.

2. **Scarcity**- If something is perceived as hard or difficult to obtain people will automatically value it more highly. Think about super bowl tickets, the latest holiday toy, advanced educational degrees, $900 per hour lawyer fees and sales/campaigns or limited time free offers. If people think (i.e. perceive) the product or service is in high demand and difficult to get (and priced accordingly) they will automatically value it more highly. Once you position yourself as a retirement income planning expert you can let your clients and prospects know that your time and expertise is valuable and in high demand. You can let them know that you are a scarce resource and your time is valuable. For example you can let them know you meet with qualified prospects by appointment only. By letting folks know that your time is valuable and that your services are in high demand, you can increase your perceived value and benefit from the law of scarcity.

3. **Consistency**- People are creatures of habit. We like things that we are used to and familiar with and tend to dislike things that are new and different. If you can show prospects how by using your product or service that it will be similar to something they already own, have experience with or are comfortable with they will be more open to your suggestions and proposals. By helping clients understand the retirement income planning process and by teaching them that building an successful income plan is like mapping out a road trip on a map for example, or creating a blueprint for a home, you can make the unfamiliar (the income plan) become familiar by discussing something that they are already comfortable with (taking a trip and using a map to get you to the destination.)

4. **Social Proof**- If you can show people that *other people like them* (same age, income level etc) are buying your product or service and that they are *highly satisfied*, it becomes easier to help the prospect make a favorable decision about your product or service. If you can show or present clients with written or verbal proof regarding how you have helped other clients

successfully create income plans, they will be much more likely to want to work with you. I'll share specific examples of social proof with you later in the book.

5. **Liking-** If people like you and if you can create rapport and a connection with them they will likely buy from you even if you have an inferior product or service. Rapport and liking are the very foundation of the sales process. That's what business lunches; golf trips and conferences are all about. Helping prospects and customers connect with vendors. If someone *does not* like you, they will *never* buy from you. Don't waste your time with them. By contrast, if they like you and your product and service makes sense to them, chances are that they will buy from you. We will cover several simple strategies that you can use with prospects and clients to easily create rapport later on in the book.

6. **Reciprocity-** When you proactively do something special or unique for someone without being asked, they will want to return the favor to you and help you with your request. Think about how you feel when someone gives you an unexpected gift for example. Chances are, you are surprised and you immediately feel obligated that you should *do something* in return for the person that gave you the gift. Even if you don't like them. The interesting thing here is that the gift does not have to be a financial one. You can give a gift of your time. You can give a gift by educating your client and providing ideas on how to reduce taxes and increase returns. Helping a client build a successful retirement income plan is the ultimate gift because it helps the client improve and enhance the quality of their life and their retirement for years to come.

So how does all of this apply to your business and the retirement income marketplace? Well unless you believe that the retirement income marketplace can represent a big part of your business going forward and unless you get excited and passionate about it, chances are you will continue doing what you are doing today and working a lot harder for less money than you would like.

In addition, when you are communicating with prospects and clients (as well as spouses and significant others) you need to know and understand how these tools of unconscious influence work and how to use them to create rapport with those that you care about (both personally and professionally.) You should try to use these in every client interaction to make sure that you connect with clients, create rapport and make them agreeable to your suggestions.

As noted above, if people think you are an **authority** or expert in the investment world you will be immediately perceived as "a cut above" other advisors in your community. You can use the tool of **scarcity** to create a demand for your services by letting prospects know your time is valuable and your expertise is sought after. You can utilize **consistency** to point our areas where clients have made mistakes in the past and to help clients recognize why it's so important to have a written retirement income plan. You can use **social proof** by writing an article, a blog or a newsletter that positions yourself as an income planning expert. You can even subscribe to services that will automatically mail your clients and prospects print or email newsletters with your signature and photo on it that gives the impression you wrote the article. You can put up and promote a financial education website. You can create rapport and **liking** by spending some time with clients and prospects and asking good questions, getting to know them and their goals and aspirations and what is most important to them in life. Finally, you can give your current clients great service and induce **reciprocity** by asking them for referrals of friends or co-workers that need to speak to a retirement income expert.

As we go through the rest of this book, you will see additional examples of how each of these unconscious tools of influence can be used and applied in a sales and retirement income planning perspective with clients.

Remember, your job during the fact-finding part of the sales process is to find out about your clients and prospects beliefs, values and core motivations.

Once you know these important factors, you can then use this information (and the tools discussed above) to help motivate and persuade your clients to buy from YOU and to use YOU as their retirement income-planning expert.

Takeaway Lessons

- **Beliefs are the foundation of excellence**. Whether you believe you can do something or you believe you can't your right.

- **You mind is like a powerful computer that records every significant life experience that you have in your life**. Just like a computer your brain decides how to feel about a certain experience and what to do about it based on the "bar codes" that get attached to a particular memory. Changing the bar code can change how you feel about something – whether it happened in the distant past, in the present or whether it will happen in the future. You can DECIDE what things mean to you and how to feel about them as a result.
- **Influence happens all the time**. You can influence behavior by making sure you manage your surroundings, appearance and references when you are meeting with prospects and clients
- The six primary tools of unconscious influence are ***authority, scarcity, consistency, social proof, liking and reciprocity.***

QUICK QUIZ- FILL IN THE BLANK

1. The _____ you make during your career and you lifetime, will impact what you think, how you feel and most importantly, how you react to the events that happen in your life.
2. Selling is all about changing a prospects _____ and putting them into a positive _____ state.
3. _____ can _____ and you can _____ them.

KNOWLEDGE APPLICATION

Answer these questions on a separate piece of paper to apply what you have learned

1. Do you have a "fear" in your life that has been holding you back from attaining your goals? Describe what the fear is and all of the *positive outcomes* that could happen in your life if you got rid of this fear right now.
2. Can you remember a time in your life when you did something extraordinary that other people said you could never do? What was it? How did it make you feel when you accomplished it?

3. What specific steps did you take in terms of mental preparation to help you accomplish the goal in #2 above? What made you stick it out in the face of all that could go wrong? Looking back on it now, was it ultimately worth it?

4. Can you remember a time when you pushed yourself even when you didn't feel like it - and you were pleasantly surprised with the result? Take a few moments to write a few paragraphs about this experience and what you learned.

5. What made you keep pushing? Was it money, prestige, ego or something else?

ANSWERS TO QUICK QUIZ.

1. The <u>Associations</u> you make... #2 Selling is all about changing a prospects <u>associations</u> and putting them into a positive <u>emotional</u> state. # 3 <u>Beliefs</u> can <u>change</u> and you can <u>change</u> them.

CHAPTER 2:
Building Your Retirement Income Brand

"Part of the planning process involves evaluating the objective, analyzing the strengths and weaknesses of the enemy and exploiting the enemies weakness and leveraging your strengths."

TOP GUN Pilot
Call Sign "Fox"

What's ahead in this chapter:

In this chapter you will learn how to develop a plan for uncovering and marketing your unique advantages so that you can create your own personal brand and clearly distinguish yourself as a retirement income expert in the marketplace. The reason for this is simple. I want your clients and prospects to understand your true value and worth. Equally important, you will learn a proven process of how to create and deliver your 'personal branding message' so that you have the maximum chance to make a positive and favorable impact on your ideal clients.

Why is this so important? Because right now there are approximately **77 Million** "baby boomer" investors out there in the financial marketplace who are looking for a qualified, capable advisor to help them make their retirement dreams a reality.

You can help them make these *critically important* investment decisions with their money.

But you and I are not operating alone in the financial services world.

There are hundreds of small, medium and large investment firms, banks, mutual fund companies, insurance firms and countless individual financial advisors out there who would like to earn a piece- or all of- this groups substantial financial business in the years ahead.

*Consider this fact. We learned earlier that it's estimated that there are **650,000 people** just like you who call themselves financial advisors or financial planning consultants- and each one of these 650,000 people is competing directly with you and your firm for client assets.*

So how does the average client distinguish you from the army of suits out there that are toting around briefcases full of investment results, pie charts and mind numbing investment statistics?

How do you get prospects to WANT TO choose you instead of choosing someone else?

This chapter will show you how.

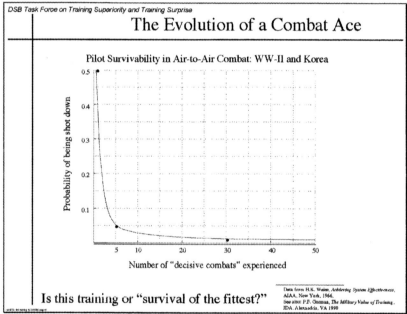

DSB Task Force on Training Superiority and Training Surprise

The Evolution of a Combat Ace

Pilot Survivability in Air-to-Air Combat: WW-II and Korea

Is this training or "survival of the fittest?"

Data from H.K. Weiss, *Achieving System Effectiveness,* AIAA, New York, 1966.
See also: P.F. Gorman, *The Military Value of Training,* IDA. Alexandria, VA 1990

Analysis of air, submarine and other combat showed that individuals who survived an engagement in which a kill was achieved were much more likely to win the next one. Until Top Gun, this was thought to be battlefield Darwinism. We now know that much of the effect is the result of to training.

The chart above illustrates the powerful impact that ongoing training can have for the average combat pilot. The basic message here is that the *more engagements* that a pilot has with the enemy, the *more skilled* they become and the *lower the chances of being shot down* in future engagements. [1]

This is what a 'learning curve' is all about. The question that sales managers and TOP GUN instructors face is *"how can I get my people to rapidly advance through the learning curve while maintaining a high level of skill, proficiency and readiness?"* That's what we will learn in the rest of the book.

In both war and in business, *preparation is power* and it can help you gain the winners edge over the competition.

In the sales and management world, clearly understanding your mission, your role in executing the mission and the strengths and weaknesses of your products and services (and your strengths and weaknesses as an individual contributor) are critically important for long term success in the business world.

More than 50 years ago, management consultant Peter Drucker started asking his clients a very powerful question. The question was: *"What business are you in?"*

Inevitably, people answered as if he had asked, "What do you *do?"*

Drucker would always stop and correct them. In the process, he proved that understanding the distinction between *what you do* and the *business you are in* is a powerful competitive advantage.

The CEO of Starbucks, Howard Schultz once was reported to have said that:

> *...We're not really in the coffee business per se, we provide a place for the local community to meet and get together ...and we just happen to serve coffee."*

Starbucks isn't in the "coffee" business, they are in the "people" business and they just happen to sell Coffee.

Coffee is a *commodity*, Starbucks is a *brand*.

Financial services products are a *commodity*, becoming an income-planning specialist creates a *brand* for you and your practice.

---

1 Report of the Defense Science Board. US Department of Defense. Training Superiority and Training Surprise January 2001.

Your Hidden Advantage- Becoming A Retirement Income 'Ace'

Imagine for a moment that you were entrusted with selecting a pilot for a very important mission during WW2 – one in which the pilot would likely be involved in aerial combat. Who would you want to select for the mission to maximize your chances for success? An average pilot -or someone like Bill Dunn who was the first American "Ace" Fighter pilot of WW2? Bill Dunn shot down 5 enemy fighters in August of 1941. There is no question that you would want Bill, or someone of comparable skill to be the obvious first choice. When people want an important job done right they look for the best-qualified people to carry out the task. ***In your business, your goal should be to be perceived as an "Ace"- the best in the business.*** You want to be perceived as the 'best' at what you do in the mind of your clients and prospects. This will *differentiate you* and increase your *perceived value* or 'personal brand' to clients and prospects. What areas of expertise should you focus on to become an expert in? This sounds like a broken record, but how about becoming known as a retirement income planning expert?

As you know by now, a "brand" is much more than a corporate logo or image.

A brand is actually a position or 'mental real estate' that a company or individual occupies in the mind of the prospect. I like to call it 'psychic real estate'

Let me play a quick game with you to help illustrate the power of branding and positioning.

1. What is Vanguard best known for?
2. How about Mercedes-Benz?
3. How about Toyota?
4. How about Ritz Carlton?
5. How about Wal-Mart?
6. How about Apple?

Chances are, you answered that these companies are best known for:

1. What is Vanguard Mutual Funds best known for?

   Low cost investing /Index mutual funds

2. How about Mercedes-Benz?

   High quality/Premium price

3. How about Toyota

   Moderate price/Great value

4. How about Ritz Carlton?

   Exceptional customer service/World class experience

5. How about Wal-Mart?

   Low prices/Wide selection

6. How about Apple?

   Innovative, fun, easy to use electronics (Computers, phones etc)

Vanguard, Mercedes and Wal-Mart have fairly clear-cut distinctive positions in the marketplace. People know what to expect in terms of quality, service or price when they interact with these firms.

An effective (but unscientific) way you can tell how strong a firm's brand is in the marketplace is to ask a few average people in the street "What does company X stand for" - if the people you ask all give you similar, short, coherent answers then this company has done a pretty good job establishing it's brand in the mind of the customer. When you think copies for example, most people think "Xerox"; when you think tissues, you think "Kleenex." Ideally, when customers or prospects think of a particular need or want that they have, you want them to think of your product (and you) first. That's what effective branding is all about.

THE $10,000 QUESTION

Let me share a quick story with you. Not too long ago I worked with a financial advisor in a local bank who wanted to become known as a retirement income-planning expert. He has a number of industry credentials, but no real marketing plan regarding how he plans to market and promote himself to his ideal clients.

One of the questions I asked him during our first meeting was the following:

"Think about the community you live in for a moment. Think about how many other financial advisors live and work within a 10 or 20-mile radius of your home or office. The number is likely to be significant.

Now answer this question. Who is the financial advisor who is best known in your community as the 'retirement income-planning expert'? Who do you know that advertises and promotes themselves this way? Who is specializing in this area? If you don't know anyone who 'owns' this piece of mental real estate in your local market, why shouldn't it be YOU?"

When I asked him these questions, I saw a look of stunned surprise on his face.

These questions peaked his interest --and motivated him to work to create his own practice-marketing plan. By using the information I will share with you in this book, I went on to formally train the advisor over a two week period on how to brand and position himself as an income-planning expert in his community.

The result? On his first retirement income planning appointment he made a **$10,000 commission** and received **4 qualified referrals** from the happy client that he had created an income plan for.

<u>This was the result from just one client and just one plan.</u>

And this example is typical rather than the exception. Done the right way, income planning can significantly boost your income and help you drive more qualified referrals in to see you.

Think of how many of your clients need a written income plan right now-- and how much money you are leaving on the table and giving to your competition right now by not being perceived as an income planning expert. It's probably much more than you think. .

OWNING A SHARE OF MIND

I call the process of understanding the associations you want to create in the mind of your target clients your *share of mind.* Another word for this might be *psychic real estate* or even *'positioning.'*

In the classic marketing book <u>*Positioning*</u> by Al Ries and Jack Trout they refer to "positioning" as <u>NOT</u> something you do to a product or service, but rather they state that *positioning is <u>how</u> you differentiate your brand in the <u>mind</u> of the prospect.*

Positioning is all about psychology and understanding how to alter and manipulate perceptions so that whatever you are selling becomes more attractive and unique.

That's what Ralph Loren does exceptionally well.

Why else would someone pay $50 or $80 for a dress shirt with a little Polo player on it?

It's not the shirt that we are buying, the materials cost about $7-- it's the brand image and how it makes the customer feel when they wear it.

Mercedes Benz, BMW and Lexus also do this very well, along with hundreds of other companies that are selling "premium" brands.

A company's brand or the position it holds in the mind of a prospect is one of the most valuable intangible assets that a company can possess. Think about what the lifetime value of the name "Coca- Cola" or "Mercedes-Benz" or "Apple" or "Ralph Loren" is. Hundreds of millions of dollars? Billions of Dollars? Maybe more?

In *Positioning*, Ries and Trout also reveal the fact that in general, people only associate one or two primary things with a particular company. They discuss the fact that the best way to get in a prospects mind is to get there **first.**

Here are a few fun examples from one of their books that validate the concept of positioning even further.

1. Who was the first person to fly solo across the Atlantic Ocean? Who was the second?
2. Who was the first person to walk on the moon? Who was the second?
3. Who was the first person to break the sound barrier? Who was the second?
4. What Boston silversmith was famous for riding to Lexington and Concord and spreading the word that "the British are coming?" Who else did this man ride with?
5. Who was the first President of the United States? How about the Second President of the United States?

The answers regarding the first people in each category are Charles Lindbergh, Neil Armstrong, Chuck Yeager, Paul Revere, George Washington and John Adams.

Almost no one remembers who the second person was in these categories. Did you? Most people remember uniqueness and the first person or product in the mind often 'sticks.'

But what if someone already owns the number one spot? If that's the case, all you need to do is to ***create another category*** you can be first in- Just like Amelia Earhart was the first *woman* to solo across the Atlantic Ocean. Lindbergh was the first, so she decided to be first at *another category (first woman)*. Paul Revere actually traveled with three other people on his famous midnight ride. Revere is remembered and the other two are largely forgotten by history because a poem written by Henry Wadsworth Longfellow was taught to schoolchildren that recounted the famous ride.

Having three characters in the poem did not work so Longfellow focused just on Revere. The rest, as they say is history. Revere was "branded" forever as the person who warned that the "British are coming"

This may not be "fair", but it's the way it is.

Here is a quick test to determine if you need to create your own personal brand --or if you should stick with what you have been doing in the past.

Think of all the prospects you have met in the last few weeks. If your manager called each of these prospects to conduct a 'customer satisfaction' survey on the appointment you conducted with them what would they say?

What if your manager asked them a question like "Can you tell me what "X" does and how he explained his role at the firm to you?"

- How would these people you just met answer your managers questions? Would they remember you?
- Would they remember what you do?
- Could they explain what you do to someone else?

If not, then we need to work together to build your personal brand and create a "bulletproof" role statement that makes an impact and is memorable so clients and customers not only remember it- but also so they can tell what you do to others.

The biggest mistake people make when creating psychic real estate is trying to have their personal brand be associated with too many things. In the investment and financial services business it's easy to want to be all things to all people. Holding yourself out as an investment expert that specializes in "sophisticated equity trading strategies, income planning strategies, life insurance planning, IRA rollovers and retirement consultations" would be very hard to articulate to a client.

You can't be all things to all people.

You need to determine **one thing** or one activity that you are really good at that you enjoy and lead with that one thing.

What if you decided today to make that one thing your expertise as a retirement income planner?

By now, hopefully I have convinced you that branding works and that good marketing can and does change customer perceptions about products and services. Now the next question is, how can you use this very same information in your own investment practice to help market promote and brand yourself as an income-planning expert?

Let's close this chapter with one additional idea that you can use and apply immediately in your practice.

CREATING YOUR PERSONAL ROLE STATEMENT

One of the first things that you need to do well in advance of actually meeting clients and prospects face to face is to develop a clear, compelling role statement for yourself. What is a role statement? My definition of a good role statement is:

> "A quick, concise description of what you do that is unique and communicated to the customer or prospect in an easy to understand, highly memorable manner"

Another word for this is an "elevator speech." This concept sounds simple, *and it is simple* but chances are that you will have to spend some time developing and preparing a few different role statements to use with potential clients. You need to spend some time in advance to develop them and get them right by testing them with real clients to see if they work - or if instead you get a blank stare. If you get a blank stare from a prospect after using one, try another variation.

By the way, creating a role statement is not something new. Good salespeople tend to use them, average salespeople tend not to. Typically, the concept of a role statement or "elevator speech" is used frequently in the venture capital (VC) business where the venture capitalists reviews dozens of potential new business ideas looking for the small handful of ideas to invest their money in.

The "elevator speech" or your role statement is designed to be delivered in a short period of time in a way that is unique and has maximum impact. Typically, this role statement should be able to be delivered by you in the time it takes for an elevator to travel from ground floor to the 20th floor of a building (hence the name 'elevator speech') If your role statement cannot be delivered quickly and concisely then it is more like a regular speech- not an elevator speech.

Let me give you an example. Imagine for a moment that you have worked hard on a new business idea for year or more and you now have the chance to 'make a pitch' for your invention to a group of potential investors to get them interested in investing money in YOU and YOUR IDEA. Let's also suppose that you could get an audience in front of these wealthy investors – and this group of people has the capability of making your dreams a reality --and maybe making you rich in the process.

How much time would you put into preparing for your presentation to this group?

Chances are that you would spend considerable time and energy preparing.

Chances are, you would be thinking about *what* you would say and *how* you would say it in a way that has the *maximum impact* on your audience.

This essential piece of your personal marketing plan is taught to MBA students at my Alma matter, Babson College in Wellesley, Massachusetts.

At Babson, they call this a "Rocket Pitch" but the purpose is very similar to the role statement or 'elevator speech' concept we have been discussing.

Whether you are trying to raise money for a new product idea or business from a skeptical venture capitalist, or whether you are trying to convince a prospect that meeting with you is worth an investment of his time and attention, the challenge is the same.

You need to quickly convince the person in front of you that *what you have to say matters,* that it is *important* and most importantly that it *will benefit them.* You have to be able to do this *quickly* in a way that is *memorable and unique* so that *you and your idea stand out* from the rest of the crowd.

Here are a few examples of basic role statements that could be used for someone in the financial services business that is involved in providing guidance and planning advice to individual investors. These examples are meant to be used simply to help you understand the structure of a good role statement so that you can create one for yourself that creates interest and is memorable and effective. You should use the process below to create and test your own role statement.

EXAMPLES OF ROLE STATEMENTS FOR RETIREMENT INCOME

1. My role at XYZ Company is **kind of like being a financial MD. What I mean by this, is** I've been trained extensively in retirement income planning and my job is to understand some of the key challenges my clients have when preparing for retirement ....and then to work closely with them to develop a personalized treatment plan to help them retire with the type of lifestyle they want.

    Key take-away message: I am your Financial MD.

2. My role at ABC Company is *kind of like being the pilot of a commercial aircraft. What I mean by this is* that I use my expertise and training to develop retirement income plans that get my clients quickly and safely to their desired destination.

    Key Take-Away message:. I will help you get to your destination safely.

3. My role at the ABC *Company is kind of like being a general contractor on a construction project. What I mean by this is* I meet with people all day long and hear about their investment goals, dreams and aspirations. It's my job to take the aspirations and dreams my clients have and turn them into reality by creating a plan or blueprint for them. Once we agree on the blueprint, we will then we work together to find specialists or 'subcontractors' to

help us complete specific tasks on the construction project. That's the way I help my customers successfully manage their money for retirement.

> ***Key Take-Away message: I'm like a general contractor for your portfolio. I'll work with a team of financial experts to help you successfully retire.***

Creating Your Personal Role Statement

As a general rule, many average salespeople do not use role statements because they are concerned that they might sound scripted or rehearsed when introducing themselves. This is a big mistake. We all know that when you meet a person for the first time you make an immediate impression of whether you like or dislike the person – often in the first thirty seconds of the interaction. Having a memorable role statement that communicates what you do in a unique manner that clients can relate to can go a long way towards creating interest and branding yourself as a true professional.

Because so few average salespeople invest the small amount of time required to create, tailor, test and refine their own personal role statement, they remain among the thousands of nameless "financial consultants", "financial planners" and "financial advisors" out there in the marketplace.

By creating and using your role statement the 'right' way, you will have taken the first step towards "branding" yourself as someone who is unique and not like everyone else.

Here is the simple formula for creating a powerful memorable role statement.

FIRST: Always begin your role statement by saying "…my role at ABC (Your company) *IS KIND OF LIKE….* and then use an analogy to explain how what you do is like something that the client is already familiar with. The potential variations here are endless. First, just spend a few minutes identifying the key aspects of what you actually do for clients. Then, think of a common experience that your customer is likely to have had or experienced in the past that can *favorably illustrate* what you actually do by analogy.

SECOND: Within the body of the role statement you want to communicate the message that you are *experienced and have unique skills.* In the examples above I used the examples of a Doctor, an Airline Pilot and an Architect /General contractor to explain the planning capabilities and service that a potential client could expect from me. You could use any profession that is _well known and respected_ to create your analogy. Obviously, it's important to use an example that people associate something *favorable to* when making the comparison.

Also, feel free to take, test, use and adapt the three sample role statements I just shared with you. They are time tested and have worked magic for me personally (and for dozens of other financial professionals) over the years. They can also work in a variety of industries- not just in financial services sales.

Of course, you can be in ANY type of sales to use a role statement. All you need to do is:

1. Identify the key things that you and your company can do uniquely well for a client. What do customers buy from you? Why? What are they looking for from you? What are the steps in the buying process?

2. Next, begin your role statement with the phrase "My role at ABC Company IS KIND OF LIKE..." and then compare what you do to something that the client is likely to be familiar with. Again, make sure that the thing you compare is something the client is likely to have a positive association with.

TAKEAWAY LESSONS

- Developing your 'personal brand' will allow you to differentiate yourself from the competition
- Clients and prospects will pay more for perceived value
- When you understand what you are REALLY selling, you will be able to rapidly increase your sales effectiveness.
- You are not in the 'product' business- you are in the relationship business. You can build powerful; long-term relationships by letting clients know that you are *much more* that a product-pusher or transaction orientated salesperson. Remember, perception is reality. If you don't like how customers and prospects perceive you, you can change the way they think about you.

- The highly valued emotional states, feelings and desires that your customers unconsciously "link" or "associate" with your products and services will determine whether or not they will buy from you.
- "Share of Mind" refers to the position your product or service holds in the mind of the prospect

QUICK QUIZ- FILL IN THE BLANK.

1. What is the Wal-Mart brand known for? More _____ at Everyday _____; Vanguard is best known for _____; Mercedes –Benz is best known for _____ and _____.
2. Car advertisements don't just sell transportation; they sell or link various attributes like S_____; A_____; P_____; S_____ and D_____. And of course, they also sell or "link" S_____ to cars."
3. If someone (another person or firm) already owns the 'psychic real estate' in a customers mind for a particular product, then all you need to do is create a N_____ C_____ to be first in. This is a way to differentiate you from the competition.
4. The definition of a good role statement is " A quick, concise description of W_____ you D____, that is U_____ and communicated to the prospect in an E_____ to U_____, M_____, manner.

KNOWLEDGE APPLICATION

1. What is one area, based on your background and knowledge that you could specialize in?
2. What are one or two words that you want your prospects to associate with you AFTER they finish meeting with you for the first time?
3. What is Wal-Mart's position in the marketplace? How about Xerox? Who owns the position for tissue paper? What does Vanguard represent? What about YOUR Firm?

QUICK QUIZ ANSWERS

1. More products at Everyday Low Prices; Vanguard is best known for Low Fees; Mercedes-Benz is best known for high quality and premium price
2. Car advertisements don't just sell transportation; they sell or try to "link" various attributes or values like Speed; Adventure; Prestige; Strength and Durability to the cars they are selling. And of course, they also sell or "link" Sex to buying a car.
3. New Category to be first in.
4. The definition of a good role statement is " A quick, concise description of what you do, that is unique and communicated to the prospect in an easy to understand, memorable, manner."

CHAPTER 3
Creating Personalized Income Plans for Your Clients

"My job is to be the best combat aviator in the world. What I mean by this is that my mission- and the mission of the team that supports me is to protect and defend the United States of America from its enemies."

-TOP GUN Pilot
Call Sign "Opus"

The description that the pilot gave above is clear and memorable. It is precise and unambiguous. Best of all, when I heard it delivered, it was communicated with power, force and conviction that left no doubt in my mind that this individual was serious. This pilot clearly understands the 'big picture' mission. He also understands the role that he and the rest of his support team plays in accomplishing the mission and making it a success.

Although the pilots receive much of the glory and take much of the front line risk, they are only one element of a much bigger team that is tasked with helping to contribute to the success of the mission. The rest of the team might include weapons officers and flight mechanics on an aircraft carrier. It might include refueling aircraft and aircrews, meteorologists, surveillance planes, intelligence analysts and the coordinated efforts of other parts of the armed services.

THE MISSION BRIEFING

Before a pilot departs on his mission, he needs to attend a mission briefing.

The overall purpose of the **mission briefing** is to map out logistics of the planned operation, plan for contingencies and to coordinate and provide the latest information available to all of the various people that have a role in the successful completion of the mission. You can have the best fighter pilot and aircraft in the world but if someone forgets to load the correct weapons on the aircraft, forgets where a refueling point is or makes a mistake programming a navigational computer then a mission can easily end in disaster.

One of the main purposes of a mission briefing is to put the odds in the pilot's favor and to make sure that mistakes like this do not happen.

During the mission briefing every element of the mission plan is reviewed in detail and the plan is updated, coordinated and double-checked to prevent potential mistakes. During a typical mission briefing, an officer will use orders, maps and overlays to explain the planned operation.

In the military, the purpose of the mission briefing is to:

1. Issue or elaborate on an operation order
2. Instill a general appreciation of the mission in all participants
3. Review the critical success factors of a imminent military operation and review logistics and coordination
4. Insure that all participants know the mission's objective and *their specific role* in accomplishing the objective.
5. Prepare for any problems they may confront
6. Actively plan for ways to overcome any potential problems.

The same basic process should be followed before a planned appointment in the sales world. You can be the most skilled salesperson in the world but if you leave for an appointment without having the right type of sales collateral, without any applications or support from your branch or home office and without the right 'branding' for who you are and what you can do for the prospect, chances are your 'mission' may never get off the ground.

In the last chapter we learned about the importance of branding, positioning and differentiating yourself in the marketplace. In this chapter, we will pull together much of the information we learned in the last two chapters and focus our efforts on learning the specific tactics and skills that can put the odds in your favor during an appointment.

I wanted to re-emphasize a few important ideas from the previous chapters that directly relate to creating your own personal brand.

1.   Effective marketing is all about *how you differentiate* what you do in the minds of clients and prospects
2.   Marketing depends *on shaping perceptions* that already exist in the mind of the customer. Where there are no existing perceptions or placeholders in the mind for a specific category or product, it's the job of good marketing to create a new perception or placeholder to fill the hole.
3.   Perceptions *can and do change*, and as a marketer it's your job to change them so that your product or service is perceived in the best light.

Before you head out on an appointment, you want to make sure that the prospect or customer perceives you as an expert that is deserving of their time and attention. One of the ways you can do that is through a personal biography, brochure or website that highlights your expertise.

I'd like to take a moment and share a few visual games with you that illustrate the power of perception and the fact that people often see what they are conditioned to see based on their past experiences. In a sense, the job of good marketing is to enable them to see not just one figure in each diagram, but many.

In the images that follow, it's likely that you may see different objects depending on your own personal background and life experiences. Some objects may jump right out at you, while others may be more difficult to perceive.

Take a few moments to look at each figure and jot down what you see next to each picture. Then, look even closer and see *what else*, if anything, you see in each picture. Each one of these figures may have at least two separate and distinct objects that you should be able to discern.

If you look for a while and still cannot see two distinct images (and if you want some help) turn to page 39 and I will tell you what to look for.

WHAT DO YOU SEE?

1. _____

2. _____

3. _____

Some Common Answers to the Perception Game.
(From left to right starting with the object in the upper left)

1. Dalmatian dog sniffing the ground <u>or</u> Leaves on the ground near a tree on a fall day
2. A profile of an old lady <u>or</u> a back/side profile of a young lady (the mouth of the old lady is a necklace of the young lady)
3. A duck <u>or</u> a rabbit
4. An Eskimo in a parka <u>or</u> an Indian figurehead
5. The word FLY in white letters against a black background <u>or</u> a water faucet.
6. A young woman looking straight at you <u>or</u> a man playing a musical instrument.

These examples are just a fun way to remind ourselves that our perceptions depend to a great extent on our past conditioning. We sometimes see only what we have been taught to see and often don't look any further. The job of a good personal biography and role statement will be to help both clients and prospects see you and your capabilities from an *entirely new and different* perspective.

The perspective of a professional and an expert vs. a generalist and a salesperson.

If you're in the financial services business (or any sales business for that matter) have you ever wondered what *the top two or three questions* are that every client is thinking about you? Have you ever wondered what could happen if you answered these questions successfully before the client brought them up? I've been searching for those key questions for much of my adult life, and as a gift to you, I'd like to share these 'Golden' questions with you now.

Here are **the three most important questions** that you need to be able to answer successfully during an appointment in order to make a sale to a customer or prospect that involves any meaningful financial commitment. If you are in real estate, telemarketing, insurance, investments, computer hardware or software sales- the line of sales you are in doesn't matter- you will still need to answer these *very same questions* successfully to make a sale.

THREE 'GOLDEN' QUESTIONS YOU <u>MUST</u> ANSWER TO GET A PROSPECT TO BUY FROM YOU

Customers will rarely come out and ask you these questions directly. But they are there in the back of their mind, right below the surface. If you answer these questions directly (or indirectly) in your presentation without being asked, this will immediately build trust and rapport with your prospect or customer.

Here are the three questions:

1. **Can I trust you?** Trust is the foundation of the selling process. Unless the prospect trusts you and believes that what you are saying is true, you will not make a sale. Without trust, when you go to 'close' you will often get the old phrase "I need to think about it." Or "I need to speak to my spouse/ significant other" When a prospect says, "I want to think about it" what they are really saying is that you have not yet convinced them of either your sincerity or the merits of your product -or both. The prospect is not disturbed enough or convinced enough to make a decision -so they put it off. To address this all important question, you should know that one of the best ways to build trust is to show clients testimonials or endorsements from other satisfied clients who have similar needs concerns as they do. Remember when we learned about 'social proof' earlier in the book?

2. The second question you need to answer is **"Are you capable and qualified to help me?"** No one wants to deal with someone who is a rookie in the business- especially if your hard earned money is on the line. So you must be able to convince your prospect that you are capable and qualified to help them solve their problems. One of the best ways to do this is to create a *printed personal biography brochure* or personal website that details your education, experience, background and credentials. You should provide this to your prospect

BEFORE you meet with them. We will discuss this a bit more in a moment.

3. The third question you must answer is **"How do you get paid?" and a related question is "What it in it for me?"** Any time you are buying something that involves a meaningful amount of money (especially where a salesperson is involved) the buyer will always want to know how the sales person is compensated. This doesn't *necessarily* mean that you need to tell the customer *how much* you will get paid in dollars if they invest a certain amount—or it might. What it means is that the customer needs to understand the *process* of how you get paid and that you are working for your benefit and theirs. You need to let them know that your interests are aligned. If you can help the customer understand that the way you get paid is linked to the wants and needs of the client, you are in good shape.

Let me give you an example. If you get paid based on customer satisfaction surveys as well as commission from a product sale, show the customer how their satisfaction has a direct bearing on your overall compensation. Show them how you both can win by working together to meet the needs and wants that the client has expressed to you.

You could also tell the customer a story and use an analogy or metaphor to explain how you get paid and say something like *"I get paid very similar to a travel agent. The company I work with pays me a fee to provide the service to you and it does not come out of your investment"*

This is a great example to use in the life insurance or annuity business where you are not obligated to disclose exactly how much you are paid but you still want to be able to address this "hidden" concern.

Another option is to come right out and say, "I charge a fee of 1% on the assets I manage subjected to a minimum investment of $500,000. For this fee, let me explain what you will receive" In the Registered Investment Advisor business you need to disclose this information anyway and you should give customers a copy of your form ADV, so come right and say what you charge and let prospects know the value added you bring to the table as a result of the fee they will pay.

Clients will also want to know 'What is in it for me?' if they are going to do business with you. They will want to know how will they benefit from the relationship. Remember, this benefit could be in the form of education, great service, expertise etc-- the *perceived value* of what you are offering must exceed the price you are charging or they won't buy. One of the best ways you can quickly and effectively answer all three of these "golden" questions is through the creation of a *high quality personal biography* or personal website. We'll discuss this next.

TELLING YOUR STORY WITH A PERSONAL BIOGRAPHY

As a salesperson, you are representing your company and the products that your company offers. The way you do this is typically verbally and through brochures and other types of sales collateral that are designed to highlight the features, benefits and advantages of working with your company and using it's products. I call this overall process of packaging your sales material, brochures and your personal biography the process of 'creating your credentials for success'

Just as important as a pen and an order blank, having the right type of sales collateral helps to reinforce the right type of image and can makes a big difference in the sales process (it also helps to create the right type of positive impression with your client or prospect.)

Just like your company and products have specific pieces of sales collateral to back up and support the sales process, YOU also need to build your credentials with clients and prospects if you want to gain their trust and business.

Some salespeople don't believe they need to formally promote their credentials-and for some salespeople, this is true. If you are selling low priced or commodity type products, it's likely that customers may not care what your credentials are. Then again, even if your product is a low priced commodity, maybe if you go the extra mile and in fact demonstrate and communicate your credentials - when your competition does not, you just might have an extra advantage in the sales process.

On the other hand, if you are selling higher priced products where the individual or corporate customer will be required to make a decision that involves a significant level of money, then communicating your credentials is essential.

The distinction between whether or not you need to communicate your credentials centers on whether you have a *transactional relationship* or an *ongoing advisory or consultative relationship.*

Almost all professional services have *consultative relationships and clients* rather than transactional relationships and customers. This is why I recommend that advisors who want to develop an ongoing relationship with clients create a personal biography that positions themselves clearly as advisors rather than just "salespeople." As I stated earlier, selling is a noble profession and you should be proud of what you do. That being said, many people have a "bar-code" in their head that associates words like "pushy" "aggressive" and "pressure" with the image of salespeople. So even though you sell for a living, rather than try to change your client or prospects existing bar code regarding salespeople, it's a lot easier to position yourself as something else- an advisor or consultant for example. That's the purpose of your role statement combined with your personal biography

Who uses a biography? CEOs, executives, doctors, academics, authors, speakers, actors, government leaders and experts in almost every field. Note that I used the word *expert* here. If you don't consider yourself an expert at what you do, then you do not need a personal biography.

Using one, however, will put you in good company. You can find numerous examples of great biographies by searching the Internet and looking up the biographies of people in leadership positions in business or government. Take a look for example at the U.S. Department of Defense Internet website and look specifically at of the personal biographies of some of the leaders and professionals that are running the U.S. military. The purpose of these biographies is to communicate the *experience, skill and expertise* that these individuals bring to their jobs as *leaders in their respective professions.*

Here is just one example of a good biography. As you read it, ask yourself the following questions.

1. Is this person someone who seems trustworthy?
2. Is this person competent and experienced?
3. Is this person experienced?

A good biography answers these three basic questions and helps you develop and frame an opinion of someone before you actually meet them.

President Barack Obama

Barack H. Obama is the 44th President of the United States.

His story is the American story — values from the heartland, a middle-class upbringing in a strong family, hard work and education as the means of getting ahead, and the conviction that a life so blessed should be lived in service to others.

With a father from Kenya and a mother from Kansas, President Obama was born in Hawaii on August 4, 1961. He was raised with help from his grandfather, who served in Patton's army, and his grandmother, who worked her way up from the secretarial pool to middle management at a bank.

After working his way through college with the help of scholarships and student loans, President Obama moved to Chicago, where he worked with a group of churches to help rebuild communities devastated by the closure of local steel plants.

He went on to attend law school, where he became the first African-American president of the *Harvard Law Review*. Upon graduation, he returned to Chicago to help lead a voter registration drive, teach constitutional law at the University of Chicago, and remain active in his community.

For illustrative and educational purposes only.

What will a biography accomplish for you? It answers most of the questions prospects and clients might have about you that they may not feel comfortable asking you directly. *Questions just like the three ones we just reviewed a few moments ago.*

A personal biography and building your package of credentials (including your personal brochure) communicates your character and competence, your skills, expertise and experience and a number of other tangible and intangible factors that enables a customer or prospect to become more comfortable with you.

In short, your biography and your personal brochure are designed to answer the most important questions prospects ask themselves before they will buy from you. The biography and role statement used together answer the questions "Can I trust you?"; "Are you qualified and skilled enough to help me?"; "How do you get paid?" And "What's in it for me?"

In our culture, most of us have been taught that it is not proper to talk about ourselves for fear of seeming self-important or bragging. As a result, in a sales context, people often say very little about themselves or their background. This is a huge mistake.

Let your personal biography do the talking and some of the up front selling for you.

Another example of a personal biography is located on the back cover of this book.

Chances are that you read this 'personal biography' of mine before you decided to buy this book. It's likely that you looked at my credentials and background, reviewed the publicity and seminar testimonials on the back cover and then skimmed through a few pages in the book when deciding whether or not, based on my background, I had something useful to say that could help you in your sales career.

So you already know that a biography works. Now we just need to create one that can do the same for you.

In many ways, the statistics that are used for athletes in baseball, football, golf, etc., serve as a quasi biography. This background information connotes ranking, skill and qualification. Your statistics determine your value, your worth and your income in sports - and the same is true in selling.

So, what are the best ways to use your personal biography?

1. You can send it to prospects *prior to* meeting them in person.

2. You can include it with your *seminar kit* at seminars you present.

3. You can use it to *introduce yourself to new accounts* that you are taking over.

Below are the four simple steps you need to follow in order to create your own personal biography brochure.

Your "biography brochure" should answer the following key questions and it should be as simple to read as possible. Avoid lots of text and make it easy on the eye to read and simple to understand. You may want to hire a professional graphic designer to do the layout for you.

Here are some questions that your **personal biography brochure** should answer:

1. How many years of experience do you have?

2. What is your position and title?

3. What makes you unique and different? (here you may want to focus on your retirement income planning experience and expertise)

4. What is your educational & professional background and certifications? (Are you a CFP or do you have other professional designations that you can highlight?)

Now that you understand how to create your own personal biography, I'd like to spend some time sharing the actual retirement income planning process with you that I have found to be both highly successful and very profitable. Before we do, I'd like to address one possible objection you might have up front.

RETIREMENT INCOME PLANNING: THE "SO WHAT" FACTOR

It's possible that you may be a skeptic about the concept of retirement income planning. Despite all we have learned so far, you might still be saying to yourself

> " *So what - all of this retirement income planning talk is just hot air. It's a myth created by marketers in the financial services industry. It won't really change my business in any significant way*"

Well, although there is a lot of marketing activity and noise around retirement income, this opportunity is REAL and it is GROWING rapidly. Many companies have not yet figured out how to fully capitalize on it yet. But they are working hard at it.

Here's why this is critically important to you and your practice.

We have all heard again and again about the tens of millions of "baby boomers" that are currently transitioning from work to retirement. What many of us are not fully aware of is the truly enormous impact that the baby boomers have had in the past on different sectors of the U.S. economy, as they have grown older.

It's important for us to look at the past to see how the baby boomers have impacted various areas on the economy so that we can get a good estimate regarding how they are likely to impact the sectors of the economy that will provide products and services to today's modern retirees.

When the troops returned from World War II in late 1945, they had one thing on their minds. They had seen terrible suffering and experienced tremendous stress and fatigue as they fought the war. They were away from their families and loved ones and when they returned home, many wanted to resume a normal life and get a good job and raise a family.

That's exactly what happened in the years following WW II. What most people were not aware of at the time was the tremendous economic impact that these baby boomers would have on the U.S. Economy. As they returned to the workforce and had families, the demand for many of the products and services that cater to the youth market grew by leaps and bounds.

As an example, the demand for baby food exploded by a factor of 10 and then by a factor of 100 by the peak of the baby boom. Other areas of the economy that experienced tremendous growth in demand for their products and services were:

- Disposable Diapers were invented in the late 1940's (is this a lucky coincidence?)
- Clothing manufactures
- Toy manufactures
- Shoe manufactures
- Bicycle manufactures
- Cartoons and child orientated movies (along with the building of Disneyland and Disney world)
- The list goes on and on....

As these babies transitioned into the ages between 5-10 during the early 1950's, the entire country saw an explosion in the construction industry as elementary and middle schools were build in every town across the country to educate these young boomers. The interstate highway system was build to help connect the country and facilitate the movement of goods, services and people.

The 1960's saw the boomers going to college and some of them going to Vietnam. The 60's also saw the civil rights movement and the mainline acceptance of "rock and roll." The summer of love, Woodstock and Vietnam war protests and the growth and expansion of the U.S. Economy during the 1950's and 60's were all driven in part by of the power of the baby boom generation making it's presence felt.

Now these 77 Million people are transitioning from the workforce to retirement. They will have very specific needs and wants during their retirement and just like the baby food and shoe industry experienced tremendous demand when the baby boomers were young, other sectors of the U.S. Economy will likely experience ***explosive growth*** as the baby boomers demand goods and services to support their retirement lifestyle.

What are some of these industries that stand to benefit greatly from the retiring baby boomers?

- **Prescription drugs.** Older folks tend to use many more prescription drugs and this sector of the economy is only likely to get larger and larger over time as new drugs are developed, tested and marketed to the public.

- **Healthcare.** Baby boomers will require medical and hospital care during their retirement years. Nurses, doctors, hospitals, home health care aids, podiatry, and many other healthcare related services will be in great demand.

- **Technology.** Today's new retirees are much more technologically savvy than their parents. They will use the internet, email, and other new technologies to stay in contact with family members, manage their money and make their retirement years more productive and enjoyable.

- **Real Estate.** Buying second homes, selling primary residences and moving to warmer climates will accelerate as the boomers seek out warm climates where they can enjoy good weather and sunshine in their retirement years.

- **Financial Services.** Boomers will have greater wealth than any generation that has come before them. They are more educated and financially astute than prior generations. Financial services firms that are able to successfully cater to and meet the investment and income needs of retirees will benefit enormously.

Knowing that the sectors listed above are likely to benefit enormously from the retiring baby boomers is like having the final scores of the super bowl before the game begins.

It can provide you with a great long-term advantage to invest a portion of your money in industries and market sectors that are likely to benefit from the retiring baby boomers. One way to benefit from this trend would be to overweight a portion of your growth orientated investments in a mutual fund or low cost variable annuity that offers sector funds in the above areas as investment options. Another way to buy into these sectors is to buy exchange traded funds.

One of the biggest challenges that the baby boomers face however, is that they have been working hard and saving money for 20 or 30 years and now they are faced with the challenge of trying to decide how to best invest their assets in a way that can provide them with both the income or paychecks that they need to fund their retirement years and the growth they need in order to sustain an income stream over a 30 year retirement.

Let me take a moment to define what an income plan is for you.

RETIREMENT INCOME PLAN

"A detailed, documented, written plan based on a client's desired retirement lifestyle that can generate both the income and growth you they will need over their lifetime."

3 Simple Steps to Create an Income Plan

So how do we create a basic income plan for a client or prospect? Simple. We want to do three things.

1. Project out how much in retirement assets a prospect is likely to have under average stock market conditions at their planned retirement date

2. Add up the prospect's estimated social security income at retirement (just ask the prospect to give you the annual statement that the social security administration mails to them or check the figures online) Also include any pension income and the

income they could receive from taking 4-5% per year out of their retirement plan balances you calculated in #1 above.

3. Compare their expected income with their essential and discretionary expenses at retirement. Essential expenses are the 'must have' items during retirement including food, taxes, housing and insurance. Discretionary expenses are everything else. The interesting thing here is different people can place different items in the essential or discretionary expense categories. Some people might think of golf as an 'essential expense' in retirement. If the essential expenses they will have are much higher than their income they will either need to save more now, delay retirement a few years or scale back their retirement lifestyle.

Once you create an income plan for a client you should revisit it annually to see if anything meaningful needs to be changed or updated based on lifestyle changes during retirement.

It's as simple as that. Once you complete the items above all you need to do is pick the appropriate (and suitable) investment products you need to implement and execute the plan. This plan might include a diversified portfolio of stocks; mutual funds or exchange traded funds and/or income or deferred annuities.

A general rule of thumb is that retirement portfolios that are designed for income planning purposes should have between 20-30% in equities (well diversified between US and international funds) and 70-80% in bond or fixed income exposure (well diversified across all maturities)

The goal here is that we are trying to create a retirement income plan for the client that balances three important objectives.

1. **Growth**- We need 20-30% in stocks or equities since if this person lives until their 90"s we need to continue to grow the portfolio over time to provide future income and to act as a hedge against inflation

2. **Predictability**- Since we will need to generate paychecks from our retirement investments, we want to have some level of stability in the paychecks that we send out to clients for paying their essential expenses like food, healthcare and taxes. Pensions and Social Security also provide predictable lifetime income.

3. **Flexibility**- Because markets change and people's goals and

needs change over time, a good income plan needs to be flexible enough to adapt and change along with the needs of the individual client.

This is a very simple way to explain retirement income planning to a client. In addition, as I mentioned earlier, the process is simple and easily repeatable throughout your client base with minimal effort.

You don't need a computer, spreadsheets, illustrations or Monte Carlo analysis to do this. You can use them if you want, but you don't have too.

Just a pen, paper and a basic calculator can help your clients create a basic plan and it will get the job done.

TAKEAWAY LESSONS

- Your role statement is a powerful tool for you to create interest with customers and prospects regarding what you do.
- There are three primary questions that you must answer for a prospect successfully before they will do business with you. Do you remember what the questions are?
- Your personal biography is your primary opportunity to leverage your background and skills in a way that position's you as an expert that can add value to the sales process.

KNOWLEDGE APPLICATION

Answer the following questions to solidify your understanding of the concepts presented.

1. What is the purpose of a role statement?
2. What is the structure of a good role statement? What phrases should it include?
3. What is the purpose of a personal biography?
4. What are the key components of a personal biography?

Next, we will examine...

CHAPTER 4
The Unlimited Power of Retirement Income Database Marketing

"For most missions, I spend 3-4 hours of pre-flight planning for every hour of planned flight"

TOP GUN Pilot
Call Sign "Cowboy"

PREPARING FOR FLIGHT

For every pilot, the planning that goes into pre-flight preparations is critical. After conducting the mission planning and the mission briefing, one of the last steps that a pilot takes before getting on the 'active' runway and taking to the air is to review a comprehensive, pre-flight checklist to make sure that they have done as much as possible (while still on the ground in advance of the flight) to prepare for the successful execution of the mission. Part of the pre-flight process might involve a final review of the destination and goal of the mission. It might involve reviewing the weapons payloads, the communications frequencies, the call signs or the locations of 'friendly' bases or airports along the planned flight path. All these small details- and countless others- including a visual inspection of the aircraft are all necessary to maximize the chances for a safe and successful flight.

The FAA has done studies over the years on civilian pilots that indicate the majority of private and commercial airline crashes have historically been related primarily to pilot error. That is, some mistake the pilot made or action that they forgot to take prior to takeoff, while in flight or during the landing process. Each year in the newspapers, we can read stories or see segments on the local television news regarding private planes being lost due to pilot error or weather.

For a pilot, training and preparation are critical since the life of the pilot and his passengers are at stake. Just like a successful pilot, adequate preparation for your appointments and client meetings is a *key factor* in predicting your chances for a successful outcome.

In this chapter you will learn:

- How to use both emotion and logic to compel your clients to buy from you.
- How to target, reach and motivate your most profitable clients.
- How to use and apply the 80-20 rule in your business.
- How to use testimonials, social proof, publicity and seminar selling to create interest and build your sales pipeline.
- How to create "instant rapport" with clients and prospects.

DOES DATABASE MARKETING REALLY WORK?

Now where does the sales process actually begin with prospects? For the most part this process begins with effective database marketing. This is the first part of the sorting process where you attempt to *create interest* regarding your products and services in the mind of the right clients and the right prospects at the right time. Effective target marketing creates a sales inquiry and the sales inquiry is the beginning of the sales process- typically driven by a salesperson. I'm going to talk about basic database marketing techniques for the financial services business, but the techniques work regardless of the industry you are in. For definitional purposes, I'd like to define database marketing as

> *"The ability to send a targeted communication to a specific group of customers that share common characteristics like age, life stage, assets and past buying habits"*

Years ago, growing up in Longmeadow Massachusetts, my family used to go to a local hardware store to buy hardware supplies. The owner of the store seemed to know every customer by name. He also knew where we lived, what my father did for work and it seemed he had an almost uncanny ability to know what we wanted to buy from him -almost before we did.

Today much of this personal touch is gone, but it has been replaced by a process that is much more sophisticated and accurate. In the sleepy little town of Conway, Arkansas, there is a firm that knows much more about you than the local storeowner of many years ago. The firm, called Acxiom, owns thousands of servers and storage devices spread across many acres. This firm is almost like the public sector equivalent of the governments National Security Agency.

The product they make is personal data.

Acxiom manages over 20 billion customer records and it maintains detailed data on the buying habits and preferences of 96% of American households. You probably aren't familiar with them, but they know you very well. The data they maintain is invaluable to marketers because it allows them to have a "real time 360 degree view of their customers"[2] The data and the data mining technology that this company gathers and develops is rumored to be actively used by the government, including the Department of Homeland Security in the war on terror.

The challenges that marketers face today is how to best use database-marketing techniques to create targeted personalized communications for hundreds of thousands of people while making these communications *appear* unique and personalized.

Database marketing can be as simple or complex as you want it to be. It can be used to generate additional sales from existing customers and it can also be used to drive new sales from prospects. It can be used to retain customers and strengthen relationships with them. It can be used to generate referrals and build loyalty. Think of database marketing as the

---

2 FORTUNE February 23rd 2004 Pg 144.

same type of process as a fisherman using a fish finder on a boat. It is a very large ocean out there and the challenge for fisherman is to 1) Locate the fish 2) Interest the fish in what they have to offer and 3) Hook the fish and reel them in. That's a tough job and technology makes it much, much easier.

When we think of Retirement Income Planning, database marketing techniques can be used to identify and target some of the following important characteristics:

- The age of your ideal income planning prospects (typically 55-65)
- The income and assets of your ideal prospects (typically 100k+; 500k Assets)
- The amount of assets in a qualified or 401(k) plan (typically $100k or more)'
- The types of marketing messages and offers that will be most effective with each group

Depending on the level of sophistication you require (and your marketing budget) you could also gather additional data on psychographics, preferences and purchase habits of your ideal prospect group in order to create the type of marketing messages that truly stick and will motivate your target audience to act. We will learn more about psychographic profiling in the next chapter.

Let me take a moment to share one basic database marketing technique with you that you likely participate in without being fully aware of how it is used behind the scenes. A few years ago the big national retail grocery store chains started using "shopping cards." These shopping cards were marketed to the public as an easy way to get discounts without the hassle of clipping coupons.

The REAL Reason for these shopping cards, however, wasn't just to make life easier for the buying public. It was to enable the store to track and build a comprehensive database of each customer and their unique buying habits.

Retail stores adopted these shopping cards slowly due to the fact that traditionally "prospects" were driven into stores by newspaper advertising in local papers that would promote sales and specials.

Beginning just a few years ago, retailers began to issue proprietary cards to frequent shoppers. In my wallet I have a "Stop & Shop" card and a "PUBLIX" card. You probably have one or two similar cards in your wallet or purse right now. But why do we *actually use* these cards? And more importantly, what *value or business opportunity* do they provide to the store?

When these cards are presented at the checkout counter, point of sale equipment (like the bar code scanners we discussed earlier in the book) permits the retailer to know *what* every household is buying, *when* they are buying it and *how much* they buy and most importantly, *what to charge* for each item. Retailers use this data to build a comprehensive database of a customer's shopping habits.

This data was (and is) extremely valuable to the grocery stores. In one recent study, after the retailers analyzed the data that they had collected from these shopping cards, **they discovered, much to their shock and amazement, that the top 20% of their customers over the course of a year spend about 50 times the amount of their bottom 20%!**

Combine this knowledge with modern Point Of Sale (POS) technology, and it becomes possible to make one offer to a frequent, high spending customer, a completely different offer to a low spending customer, and yet a third offer to a new customer with moderate spending habits.

For example, every time I use my PUBLIX or Stop & Shop card, I am given certain discounts on products to induce me to provide my card to the teller upon checkout. As a result of my using my card, the store knows that I purchase baby food, diapers, rib-eye steaks, and a wide variety of other products on a regular basis. All of my purchasing patterns are stored in a vast database and analyzed on a periodic basic. As I pay the for my groceries at checkout, the computer will offer me a series of additional coupons to be used on *future visits* that are based on my past purchasing history and the items that the store wants to promote or sell. The computer then spits out some instant coupons for me on the back of the receipt I am given.

Interestingly enough, the coupons are always for something directly or indirectly related to my actual needs or wants. Next, in the following weeks I might get a wide variety of offerings through the mail for baby and children related products.

EXAMPLE: USING DATABASE MARKETING TO YOUR ADVANTAGE

Here's the power of this.

Let's say you have older teenage children and your weekly grocery purchasing habits reflect this. If you use a shopping card, then unlike the offers I might get with young children, <u>you</u> will get *different offers* targeted to *your unique needs* and wants. The offers that you receive will be based primarily on *your past purchasing habits* stored in the customer database. These shopping cards will enable the store to offer you the products you are most likely to buy, at the right time and at the right price.

This saves the store millions of dollars in annual advertising expenses and allows them to focus targeted, customized offers to each individual shopper.

That's the power of database marketing.

Now, think for a moment about your most profitable clients. What professions are then in? What is their income and asset level? What age are they? What do they do for leisure activities? As you start to think about this, chances are that you will begin to see some very specific patterns regarding what types of clients are your best clients. With database marketing, you can find dozens—maybe hundreds of clients that look just like them. **Database marketing can dramatically speed up your sales cycle, reduce the time you spend prospecting and increase your profits.**

These programs, just like airline frequent flyer programs and hotel rewards programs are all database marketing systems designed to build customer loyalty and drive incremental sales. These programs also recognize the fact that all of the customers that walk into the store, fly on an airline or visit a hotel <u>*should not*</u> be treated equally and that they should be <u>*rewarded differently*</u> based on the volume and nature of purchases that they make.

If you stay in a Marriott hotel for example and you use their rewards card, you might accumulate a certain number of points based on the number of nights you spend at a hotel and how much you spend each time you stay. Then you may get special offers and upgrades, additional discounts, free nights, or free dinners at the hotel -or other hotels in the Marriott chain. You may also get other periodic offers designed to build your brand loyalty and boost the amount of money you spend each time you visit.

In a sense, marketers have realized that by focusing a portion of their marketing efforts on *existing customers* they are able to make much more money by selling to people who *already have* a relationship with the firm - and as a result many companies are spending less on "shotgun" advertising designed to draw in random new prospects.

During my time at Fidelity, the company spent considerable sums of money on database marketing and customer relationship management programs. In recent years, more and more money has also been spent on targeted "customer appreciation" functions that are designed to reward and motivate existing customers with significant assets that do business with the firm. The objective, of course, is to thank customers for the past business, to build the relationship with these clients and to encourage them to do more business with the firm in the future.

These customers might be offered a private event or seminar with a Fidelity portfolio manager or perhaps an upscale dinner and seminar presentation designed to thank them for the relationship they have with the firm.

The company might also decide to provide extra perks, service levels and incentives to customers based on the amount of assets that they have at the firm, how frequently they trade stocks or how long they have been a loyal customer.

Now, just taking care of *existing customers* is one part of the equation. The other part of the equation is prospecting for *new households* or prospects that look just like your most profitable customers from a demographic and psychographic point of view. Prospects who may be doing business currently with your competition. The goal, of course, is to get them to do business with you and your firm.

Fidelity, and many other banking, brokerage, insurance and mutual fund firms have active programs to support these key objectives of acquiring new households and building relationships with existing customers. In today's world, if you're serious about your business you simply can't survive in the long run without programs like this.

So you might be asking yourself, what if I don't have the resources of a big financial services firm? You might be wondering if there is still a way that you can easily and economically use database-marketing techniques to drive business from your existing customers and prospects.

The answer, of course, is YES there is a way. Next I'll show you how.

THE 80-20 RULE FOR RETIREMENT INCOME- DOES IT STILL APPLY?

We just learned that large supermarket chains realized to their amazement that the **top 20%** of their customers spend on average **50 times** the amount as the bottom 20% of their customers. In sales there is an old reliable rule of thumb that I am sure you may have heard of. It's called the "80-20" rule and what it means is that on average 80% of your revenue and sales will likely come from the "top 20%" of your customers.

A few years ago the former Treasury secretary and former CEO of Goldman Sachs, Henry Paulson made a statement that articulated the "80-20" rule quite well but he angered and offended many of his co-workers in the process. When speaking about issues of corporate productivity and pending layoffs, he said, *"There are 15-20% of the people who really add 80% of the value. Although we have good people, you can cut a fair amount …and still be well positioned for the upturn."*[3] Although this was politically incorrect to say in a speech, it clearly articulated and validated the fundamental law that on average, the top 20% of the people often generate 80% of the results in life. The same is true in sales, management, sports, and a wide variety of other disciplines.

Here is the real magic of the 80-20 rule as it applies to selling and customer relationships.

Most salespeople spend just as much time trying to get a sale from the 80% of 'average value' customers as they do to the 20% of customers that generally make up 80% of their sales or commission revenue.

As a salesperson, if you have a good marketing team supporting you, you typically will have *limitless prospects* and *limited time* in which to

---

3 Business 2.0 January/February 2004 Page 78.

pursue them. This creates a dilemma. How should you best spend your time and with whom? Here are a few thoughts on this.

At its most basic level, to begin, you should take a few hours and complete an analysis of where the bulk of your fee based or commission income or revenue came from last year. You don't need to wait for your firm or your manager to do this for you-you can do it yourself and you can get started NOW. All you need to do is ask yourself the question *"Who were the customers and key accounts that generated the bulk of my revenue last year?"* If you sell to individuals, what is their age and where are they in their life stage? Do they have common demographic characteristics? Do they have common beliefs and attitudes? Do they have common needs and wants? This will provide you with two critical pieces of information.

First, if customers and prospects that have the same type of profile generate 80% of your fees or commissions, then you should spend 80% of your future or current marketing efforts and sales skills talking to these folks exclusively.

This type of analysis can also help you refine your role statement and personal biography that we discussed in the last chapter. If you know who your best and most profitable customers are, if you know the products and services they buy from you most often and WHY they buy them from you, you can reflect this information in your role statement and personal biography so that you appeal to more people who are just like them.

Second, if the 80-20 rule holds true for your existing customer base (and chances are it will) then you now also know whom you want to *scale back on* in terms of your personal sales efforts. Spending *less face-to-face time* on the customers that buy *small quantities* and take up the *same amounts* of time, energy and effort as your big customers makes a lot of business sense in the long run.

You can still contact these folks, but you can do it through *passive marketing strategies* and other distribution channels that do not require a face-to-face interaction (like customer newsletters and periodic email campaigns with specific, targeted offers for example) This way you still remain in contact with these customers and *they will call you* if an idea or offer that you send them peaks their interest. This way you can focus more of your personal one-on-one selling on the top 20% of your customer base that makes the most difference - both for you - and your firm's bottom line.

Let me share a personal example of how this works. Before my time at Fidelity, I was an independent broker and advisor registered through LPL Financial services.

One year as part of my new years resolution, my brother and I agreed on and decided to do an analysis of the customers, the products and the methodology by which we did business during the previous year. We pulled out all of our old commission statements from the previous year and started to build a matrix that helped identify *which customers* did the most business with us, *the products that they bought* and *how we had marketed to these folks* to bring them on as clients.

Here is an example of whom our revenue came from and which products generated it:

Demographics	% Of Commissions revenue
Customers age 25-50	1%
Customers age 50-60	15%
Customers age 60+	84%

+++

Products	% Commission revenue
Variable Annuities	30%
Fixed Annuities	40%
Stock Trading	-0-
Mutual Funds	10%
Managed Accounts	15%
Fixed Income Buyers	5%

+++

Marketing method	% Commission revenue
Referral from existing customers	25%
Advertising	3%
Direct mail	5%
Seminars	67%

+++

For our 300 clients, this analysis took us about an hour and a half to complete in total. Here is the value of doing this. It ended up *fundamentally changing* the way that we did business going forward.

Does anything jump out at you from the analysis above?
- Who was our most profitable demographic group for us based on age?
- What types of products and services did these people tend to buy?
- How did we acquire these "ideal customers?"

Here is what the information told us about our business in a clear and powerful way:

Pre-retirees and retirees were the people that we worked most effectively with. From a time, money and staffing perspective, it did not make sense for us to focus on young emerging investors (age 25-50) since they took up a lot of our time and did not contribute much to our bottom line. This one observation by itself would save us a great deal of time, energy and effort in future years by pointing us *away from* this group and towards our most profitable group.

Variable annuities, fixed annuities, mutual funds and managed accounts represented the bulk of the products that we sold. We decided to specialize in these areas going forward and to concentrate and focus our marketing and sales efforts on annuities and managed accounts because this was where the bulk of our revenue came from. We also stopped pro-actively offering fixed income investments like individual bonds or individual stocks to customers. Here is the key. We could *still offer everything* that we offered before, but we decided to *focus on promoting our most profitable products to the right people the right way.*

The data also showed us that **seminars and referrals** were the #1 way that we had brought new faces and clients into our firm. Often, we would meet prospects at a seminar, take them on as clients, do some financial planning work with them and then later on we would typically get a number of referrals to one of their friends or business associates. We targeted our seminars on employee groups and retiree associations where there were very minimal up-front marketing costs.

As a result of this analysis, we stopped doing expensive newspaper advertising and avoided costly direct mail programs altogether.

This process is extremely simple and basic and does not cost anything except a few hours of your time. When you consider how much you spend each year on advertising, direct mail and seminars, doesn't it make sense to do this type of analysis BEFORE you spend any new marketing dollars?

You can do this very same process with your current book of customers. Simply block off a few hours of time and review three things.

Take out your year-end commission or revenue statement and ask yourself:

1. Who are my most profitable customers? What attributes do they share in common?

2. What are the product offerings that customers are buying that contribute the most to my personal bottom line?

3. How did I get in front of these profitable customers in the first place? What specific marketing method was used to turn these prospects into clients or these clients into repeat buyers?

My recommendation is that you start to use and apply these basic database-marketing concepts to your investment practice today—and focus your efforts on attracting and retaining retirement income planning clients. They will be your most motivated and most profitable clients.

Here is the bottom line: Database marketing can help you better identify and profile your customers so that you can make selling additional products and services to them easier and more productive. It can help you manage sales programs and promotions so that you can attract new prospects. It can help you better focus your sales and marketing efforts towards specific needs and wants that your customers have - and it can help you generate more sales with less overall effort and work.

If you are not using these techniques right now, you need to start using them as soon as possible.

You can begin by doing a quick analysis of the business you did last year.

USE SALES AIDS TO MAXIMIZE YOUR IMPACT

This brings me to the topics of sales aids, brochures and testimonials. The purpose of all three of these items is to do one primary thing. The purpose is to facilitate the sales process by telling the "product" story to a prospect or client that highlights the key advantages of your product or service and what the customer can expect from you if they buy your product.

As we learned in the last chapter, a personal biography brochure is designed to tell YOUR personal story and to build your credentials as an expert in your field.

The pieces of marketing collateral that you use during your sales presentation must work together to provide one unified and consistent message to the prospect.

I'm not going to spend a lot of time discussing product brochures because every product category you sell may be different and require slightly different marketing materials from a support perspective. If you are in the financial services business, for example, and you offer mutual funds, fixed income products, limited partnerships and insurance to your customers then you likely have specific brochures that the companies your work with paid for that explain each of these products. And as we all know, the brochure, no matter how well designed and how many nice photos it has in it, does not sell the product, YOU do.

That being said, to more effectively sell yourself to prospects, you should consider creating a professional looking three ring binder that you can use with customers to walk them through your personal biography, the types of customers you work with, and key testimonials or 'letters of reference' from other satisfied customers that you have worked with in the past. If you just put this 3 ring binder together, I'm certain that this sales aid will become one of your most powerful sales tools.

It will also put you ahead of 95% of the competition who has not yet spent the time to develop their own 3-ring binder.

Just remember to get legal or compliance approval for these items in advance.

THE POWER OF TESTIMONIALS

What is a testimonial? Simply put, a testimonial is an endorsement of a product or service by someone who has used the product and service in the past and is willing to 'go on record' with their thoughts. Testimonials can be in video, audio or written format.

Have you ever wondered why otherwise seemingly rational corporations in the United States and throughout the world spend hundreds of millions- even billions of dollars - paying celebrities to recommend or endorse their products? The simple reason is that testimonials work to influence behavior.

But what if you're not a celebrity and if you can't afford to hire one to endorse your product or service, what are your options?

Here is what you can do.

For years prior to my career with Fidelity, I build up both my financial service business and my sales training business by collecting a letter of recommendation from satisfied clients that I had worked with (As you might imagine, it helps to use testimonials from satisfied clients)

If a client is particularly satisfied with the work you have done, ask them if they could send you a letter of recommendation highlighting the service you have provided to them. You can even offer to type up the letter for them and ask them to review it and sign it if they agree with it. The easier you can make it for them, the better.

Over the years I have collected hundreds of these letters from satisfied clients and each one of these letters went into my three ring binder and became part of my sales presentation.

Here are a few examples of "testimonial letters" from my sales training business that were designed to generate interest and address potential objections for one of the motivational seminars I used to present.

This seminar was called (quite appropriately) *TOP GUN-The Firewalk Experience*. The seminar was designed to be a motivational seminar, but it also taught many of the powerful sales ideas and techniques discussed in this book.

Dear Scott,

I just wanted to take a moment to say thank you for the program you conducted for EMC's international sales meeting at the Ocean Edge resort. Without a doubt, the program was one of the most unusual and successful programs I have ever attended at EMC. I believe all of us who attended the meeting left the event feeling highly motivated and positive about themselves, about EMC, and about our future success.

Congratulations on a job well done. I have already begun to spread the word about your program, but please feel free to use me as a reference.

Very best regards,

Karen A. Glynn
International Field Marketing Manager
Open Storage Group
EMC

Dear Mark and Scott :

Many thanks to Peak Performance Development for making a significant contribution to the success of our Pitney Bowes Management Services' *Summit Club* sales incentive trip held in Puerto Rico in April of 1995;

The workshop you conducted as part of our business meeting session, culminating in "The Firewalk Experience" was one of the more unusual and successful programs we have done for our sales people. Your program fit very well with the theme of our conference, which was all about helping people breakthrough to the next level of success. We were very pleased that what we had originally considered to be a "risky" undertaking, was handled in such an educational, professional manner. And as the workshop evaluations showed, our people definitely enjoyed and learned from the experience.

The Magnacca brothers are quite a team - - stay in touch, and keep up the good work.

Sincerely,

John B. O'Mahoney

Mr. Scott Magnacca
Peak Performance Development
182 West Central Street
Suite 203
Natick, MA 01760

Dear Scott:

Thank you! Your firewalking presentation was the hit of our
recently concluded General Managers' Meeting on Thompson Island.
The energy and enthusiasm I witnessed was overwhelming and
something I will never forget.

I am most impressed that over 100 people participated in the event,
including our President, Jack Nugent.

As I travelled our stores following the meeting, I was struck by
the lasting impression that the event had and how "enthusiastically
confident" our managers are that they can conquer any challenge
that comes their way during our critical holiday selling season.

Once again, thanks for the outstanding job, and I look forward to
working with you in the future.

Sincerely,

Michael Wedge
Sr. Vice President
Director of Operations

Scott, Mark & Dave:

I wanted to personally thank each of you for your enthusiastic and professional delivery of "The Unlimited Personal Power" Seminar on the evening of October 13 to a very select group of experienced high achieving managers within the Chase Manhattan organization in Rochester, New York.

During the seminar each individual was challenged to walk across a 10 foot bed of hot coals (1200-2000 degrees). This of course was optional...but each manager did firewalk. The personal sense of accomplishment is extremely difficult to express in words, but overcoming fear, tapping into your inner strength and the sense that you can achieve anything was the overwhelming result.

I have absolutely no reservations in recommending this type of training experience to others. This program deals with personal power, inspiration and above all challenging yourself to conquer your inner personal fears. The Firewalk experience is something you carry with you internally for a long time . . . maybe forever.

My compliments to Peak Performance Development!

Respectfully,

Denise Selak
Vice President
Senior Management Development Specialist

Dear Scott,

I'm very sorry it has taken me so long to write to you regarding our responses to the program you presented to us last November. This delay is no reflection on your program, nor was I waiting to measure the response. I've just been very busy and you haven't bugged me too much. Thanks.

Your program was the only thing I was willing to try in my effort to top the program we last presented. It lived up to our every expectation and more. You convinced a room of 45 men and women that they could do anything they believed they could do and then had them demonstrate that belief to themselves. That demonstration is where "the rubber meets the road" in the training field and your program left "screeching tires" that none of them will ever forget. While their comments were predictable, they were just as genuine. "No one could have convinced me that I could do that." "After that, I can do anything." "I really didn't want to try, but I'm so glad I did." "I will never forget this as long as I live." "I can't believe I really did that." "I guess I really can do what I set my mind to do."
etc., etc.

I would recommend your program without reservation. It has a very strong message about every aspect of life that everyone can benefit from.

Good luck to you two guys. I hope we get to work together in the future.

U. Smith

Mike Smith
Director of Training

TESTIMONIALS ARE 'SOCIAL PROOF'

The reason testimonials are so important is they help to address the three key questions that we discussed earlier in the book. If you remember, those are the three questions that need to be answered before a sale can take place.

Testimonials can directly address the "Can I trust you?" and "Are you qualified, competent and capable of helping me?" questions.

A series of testimonials from satisfied customers can also serve to back up and support the information on your personal biography. Now of course, in the financial business the SEC does not allow "testimonials or endorsement's" regarding performance or specific investment products. **That's because they work to influence behavior and decision-making.** So if you can't use a "testimonial" maybe you can share research findings from your customers, seminar attendees or current clients that speak to your expertise, professionalism and customer service. Check with your friendly compliance person to see where the boundaries are and what specific disclosures you need for yourself and your firm.

If you look at the science behind testimonials, they are a powerful form of 'social proof' that function to take much of the fear and uncertainty out of the buying process for prospects. Remember, when people are unsure of what they should do, they often look to the behavior of *other people* who are like them to help them make a decision and decide what they should do. Testimonials can help prospects make decisions by taking some of the *perceived risk* out of the buying process. In addition to the questions above, the number one question most people have when they are about to make a new purchase is "will what I am buying work and perform as advertised?"

Good testimonials answer this question as well.

In the examples above, the sales training and motivational seminars I was promoting and selling to Fortune 500 companies early in my career were among the most challenging and difficult products that I have ever sold. Despite this challenge, the testimonials made the sales process almost effortless. Here's why.

Imagine your sales task is to convince a major Fortune 500 company to hire you to speak to its top executives, salespeople and senior managers.

Let's also suppose that for this few hours of work you will be asking for a 5 figure speaking fee.

Let's take it one step further.

Let's also suppose that as part of the motivational seminar you are going to get <u>all</u> of the meeting attendees- the CEO of the company, the senior leadership team, the managers and the salespeople to WANT TO *willingly* take off their shoes and walk across a glowing bed of 1200 degree red hot coals in their bare feet.

The 'red hot coals' I am referring to are what happens when you build a nice, big fire in your fireplace and over time watch as the fire burns down into red hot glowing embers.

Those are the red hot embers that I would need to get people to WANT TO walk over in their bare feet.

Now why would anyone in his or her right mind want to do this and pay for the privilege? Here's why.

They aren't paying for the fire walk. That is the *easy part* of the seminar. They are paying for the training and conditioning process that happens in the hours <u>before</u> the participants actually walk out on the red-hot coals.

Consider this. If this training process that participants go through can help them easily and quickly change their associations about walking on hot coals and get them to *enjoy the process* rather than fear it, think about how it could help salespeople, managers and marketers change their associations about meeting and exceeding seemingly impossible business goals?

This is the very same type of mental conditioning process that a TOP GUN pilot or a Navy SEAL goes through that enables them to push themselves beyond where they think they can go and reach higher levels of performance.

Just like at a college, you spend four hard years (for most people) looking forward to graduation and seeking the diploma, but what you are *really paying for* is the knowledge and experience that you gain in the years leading up to graduation. The diploma is a piece of paper- but *the personal life experiences are priceless.*

The fire walk is simply a fun, exciting, and very powerful and long lasting metaphor that helps people break through self imposed limits and barriers in their life.

It teaches people in a very direct and tangible way that they can do more, achieve more and create more in their life than they may have ever dreamed possible.

It helps create a new belief in individual capabilities and it inspires people to try new things, to take calculated risks and to reach for big 'audacious' goals.

That being said, think of the potential objections and concerns that would come up when trying to sell an event like a firewalk!

The reputation risk for the company.

The "Image" and public relations risk for the company (i.e. What would the press and shareholders think if they found out we were spending their money on an event like this?)

The Legal risk for the company (what if someone gets hurt, burned or worse?)

And of course, the risk that the event would be a flop or the speaker would be boring and not motivating.

If left unaddressed, these potential 'hidden' objections could create a huge boulder on the 'reasons to avoid buying' side of the decision making scale.

Obviously, any one of these risks by itself it left unaddressed could kill the sale. The reality was, however, that due in large part to the brochure and powerful testimonials or "social proof" that we showed to prospective customers (and the way we packaged, sold and positioned this event) we had more business than we knew what to do with.

Certainly, selling an event like this didn't rely on any real logical reasons to buy (there weren't any), like most sales; this event relied on selling *emotional reasons*, not logical ones.

Through the sales process, we were able to 'link' our prospect's most desired goals and outcomes for a meeting or conference to our seminar program. Once that linkage was established, the sale was accomplished.

Once we sold the program then we delivered by consistently exceeding expectations.

Finally, we asked for and received a letter of recommendation from our satisfied clients.

Remember, people are generally risk adverse and don't like to take big chances.

A good testimonial goes a long way towards eliminating that risk and nervousness by communicating the fact that you and your product and service can be trusted, that you are an expert and a professional and that the customer experience that other buyers had was excellent (or at least above average.)

I attribute much of this success we had in selling this program (and other related seminar programs we offered) to the carefully crafted testimonials and the strong relationships we developed with past clients who would gladly speak to other companies on our behalf.

In a similar fashion, when I started out in the financial services business I had no clients, no money, very little experience and fortunately a lot of motivation to succeed in the business. The way I was able to build my financial business was very similar to the way I built my sales training business. The way I did this was by offering to present free financial planning seminars for state agencies and associations throughout Massachusetts. The reason I ended up doing seminars for these folks was, quite honestly, because no one else wanted to talk to them and I noticed a marketing opportunity that I could take advantage of. In addition, early in my career I didn't have a lot of clients to talk to so I was happy to have an audience, even if they did not have lots of money. Fortunately, this situation changed dramatically over time and soon I had more qualified people to talk to than I could handle.

In Massachusetts in the early 1990's the Governor of the Massachusetts, William Weld downsized state government, closed and reduced the size of many state agencies and eliminated several thousand state jobs over a two year period. Since I didn't have any other clients to work with early in my career, I decided to *become an expert* in the intricacies of the state pension plan and I approached several state agencies offering to do seminars that would teach employees about their retirement options. It took me about two weeks of research to become an expert on the state pension system.

No one else was holding seminars for these employees so these events became a powerful way to differentiate myself and my products and services from the competition.

I started off in a state hospital in Rutland, Massachusetts and did one of my first presentations. Right after the presentation, and not really knowing any better, I boldly asked for (and received) a letter of recommendation from the Director of the hospital.

In the following weeks, I then used this letter of recommendation (with permission) to open the door for me at *other state hospitals* throughout the state. **This one letter served as "social proof" and communicated the fact that I was a specialists, that I was a good, dynamic presenter, that I did not push products in my presentation and most important of all, that I could be trusted and that I had something valuable to say to state employees.** Over a period of the next few years, my brother and I personally spoke to several thousand state employees and took on many hundreds of state employees as clients.

All of this happened as a result of noticing an opportunity and finding a way that I could differentiate myself and add value. The same is true with income planning today. It's a way to get noticed as an expert, to differentiate yourself and to adding value by offering something virtually everyone needs but very few advisors know how to deliver on effectively.

It's easy. Start by doing one simple plan for a client and getting *just one* letter of recommendation.

After you get the first one, keep on going- the rest will be easy. Before you know it you will have a three ring binder full of them. Best of all, if you use these letters the right way they will be more valuable and profitable to you than a treasure chest full of gold bars.

Here is what I suggest. Contact your local annuity or mutual fund wholesaler for the firms where you do business and ask if they will split the cost of presenting a retirement income seminar for you. They may be able to provide you with a compliance approved seminar, a speaker and funding for an actual event with clients and prospects. Once you do just one successful seminar, get a letter of recommendation from the wholesaler and use a seminar survey to get feedback from attendees. You can then use these testimonials to build of your library of testimonial letters.

SUCCESS WITH SEMINAR SELLING

As you have just read, one of the most powerful and effective ways to combine client education with selling in a multiple person format is through seminar selling. In a seminar-selling format you are able to communicate with dozens- maybe even hundreds of potential prospects at the same time. This is much more efficient than meeting customers one on one for a first appointment. In addition, seminar selling can allow you to use and apply many of the ideas and techniques that we have learned so far in this book. In your seminar introduction you can use your role statement to explain what you do in a powerful and memorable way. You can review your background and qualifications (your personal biography) in the early part of the seminar to create interest and engage the audience.

Seminars should be designed to be educational, entertaining and <u>not</u> have any strong product promotions within them. **Bottom line: You don't want to push products in an educational seminar.** You want to provide *just enough information* so that attendees start asking questions and want to take the next logical step to get help after the seminar. *Typically, in the financial services business, the next logical step would be an appointment with you, a qualified advisor.*

When I was in my own business, I would do one seminar each month for approximately 50 people each time. Between 50-75% of the attendees would want a personal follow up meeting with me --and it would typically take me 3-4 weeks to follow up with all these customers for a first and second appointment. By the time I was done, it was time to present another seminar to a "fresh" group of prospects.

Now you might be asking yourself if you could actually present a seminar yourself. Statistics show that more people fear speaking in public than fear death. The good news here is that you don't need to be Tony Robbins. If you don't want to give the seminar have an expert do it for you (maybe your wholesaler) I would however encourage you to become skilled at presenting to groups. *Because so many people are fearful of presenting a seminar in front of a 'live' crowd, you will be in very select company if you can get yourself to actually do it.* In fact, just by getting into the seminar business and speaking in front of a crowd, you will easily beat out 95% of your likely competition.

Just conducting and presenting a seminar differentiates you and puts you in a very small, unique category of sales professionals. It effectively communicates your skill, qualifications and expertise as an advisor.

There are a number of companies in the financial services business that sell "pre-packaged" financial seminars with scripts, slides, sample newspaper ads and everything that you would need to conduct a successful seminar-except for the speaker.

If you have never tried seminar selling, I would recommend that you try it if it makes sense for the business you are in. If you are concerned with costs, I suggest you talk to your friendly wholesaler for help and support. If you do business with them they are likely to help you out.

Don't get discouraged if the first few times you present a seminar you don't get a 10 out of 10. It will take time. My first seminar presentation was an accident. One of my mentors in the business had agreed to do the presentation for me. My job was just to greet the attendees and sign them in. At the appointed time for the seminar, my "mentor" was nowhere to be found. We waited, 5 minutes, then ten minutes. No show. So I had to get up and I did the presentation myself from memory. It was scary and I was nervous, and it definitely had room for improvement- but I did it successfully and the audience actually liked it.

I now had a new bar code, a new reference, and a new association in my head about seminars. I could do it! As it turned out, my "mentor" was stuck in traffic for two hours on the highway behind an overturned truck. Just like we learned earlier though, everything happens for a reason and the "bad news" was actually "good news" in disguise because this *one key experience* helped me gain the confidence I needed to do a seminar presentation myself. Once I did it myself, just one time, I realized that it was a lot easier than I had imagined it would be. This one experience and the 'positive association' that I linked up to it in my head is directly responsible for virtually all of the seminar related work that I have done in the last 20 years. During this time period, many tens of thousands of prospects have been exposed to the seminar content and presentations that I have developed and presented.

All of this happened as a result of *one experience*. One decision. The rest, as they say, is history.

If you are giving a seminar and someone does ask a question that you can't answer (or if it would take more time than you want to devote to answering it effectively) write the question on an easel under a category for "parking lot questions"- these are questions that will require in depth explanation or questions that you will research for attendees after the seminar is concluded. This way your seminar will not get disrupted and you maintain control.

Here are a few additional tips you can use when making presentations to groups of any size. First, as I mentioned earlier, just because you are a good salesperson, doesn't mean that you can easily and automatically get up in front of a room full of complete strangers and motivate them to listen to you and to want to do business with you.

In order to get them to listen to you, your presentation should be **scripted, planned out and rehearsed** well in advance. Don't 'wing it' or you will likely crash and burn. You need to be an expert on the topic you are discussing- at least to the extent that you know more about it than the audience members in front of you.

You should use slides and props to reinforce what you are saying and they should used to remind you where you are in the presentation, but you should not read off the slides directly as you present.

Second, you should build your presentation on ideas and themes that people are likely to agree with and themes that they want to learn more about.

Let me give you an example. A book I wrote a few years ago for individual investors is entitled *"The 7 Strategies for A Successful Retirement."* A companion seminar program was developed from the content of the book, which centered on key ideas that almost everyone can relate to. The idea is that *everyone who invests* money wants to *invest successfully*. In addition, everyone that is working hard and saving aggressively today, is doing so because they want to have a safe, secure, and *successful retirement.* No one wants to have an 'unsuccessful' retirement and end up living with relatives or out on the street because they don't have enough money to sustain their lifestyle. The *7 Strategies for A Successful Retirement* Seminar teaches investors in the years approaching their retirement *the seven specific steps* that they can take to *successfully* retire.

The entire seminar was built around this simple core theme and the seminar was designed to tell investors just enough so that they wanted to come in for a follow up appointment

One of the other seminar programs my team and I created was responsible for helping Fidelity test, communicate and validate some of the key concepts of retirement income planning in the retail marketplace. The name of the seminar program was *"5 Golden Rules for Retirement Income Planning"*

This was Fidelity's first experience taking the retirement income planning process "mainstream" and presenting it to retail investors in a seminar format.

Over the years this seminar content reached hundreds of thousands of Fidelity customers and prospects via the web and in live format. It also created tens of thousands of qualified appointments for Fidelity's branch financial representatives and resulted in billions of dollars of new assets flowing into the firm after we conducted the program nationally.

The seminar and the marketing program all followed the basic structure I am about to share with you.

This process has been tested and proven highly successful with affluent clients.

It can and will work for you as well.

A good seminar, then, is centered on a common truth or key theme that most people can understand and buy into. Here is the simple **5-Step formula** I use for building powerful and effective seminars:

1. Find the **common truth or key theme** that most people would agree with or are interested in. For example some common themes one could consider building a seminar around are reducing taxes, increasing returns, lowering risk. Just look at the cover of Money magazine each month for ideas on what the general public is interested in learning about.
2. Talk about the **people or the process** that you or your

company uses to help people achieve the common truth mentioned above. That is, how can you help investors become more successful at investing or reduce their risk or reduce their taxes for example.

3. Talk about or use a **case study** of how real people have followed or used this process to create 'success' in their own lives.

4. Use **interesting facts, famous quotations and/or stories** to bring the examples you use 'to life' in the seminar

5. Leave your audience **'hungry' for more**. Educate and politely disturb them, but don't give *everything* away in the seminar. The purpose of any good seminar is to create interest and motivate people to want to take the next step with you (typically a follow up appointment) If you give it all away, they don't need to come back to see you.

Also, don't forget to collect seminar evaluation forms from attendees expressing what they liked and did not like as well as their personal contact information. This information should go right into your contact management system for follow up. Remember, if you don't want to create a seminar, you could also ask your friendly wholesaler to come present a public seminar for you or even buy a legally approved seminar off the shelf.

So these are the **5 basic steps** that I use to **build successful seminar programs**. Many other presenters use the same (or a similar) formula.

If you want to present seminars effectively, you will need to spend a minimum of a few days rehearsing before you present your first seminar. Read the seminar script. Talk through the script out loud -and if you can- actually go through a rehearsal or mock presentation with the actual slides and your equipment in the days leading up to your seminar. Remember, professional actors all rehearse numerous times before the camera starts shooting. You should do the same if you want to make the most powerful impact you can.

THE POWER OF PUBLICITY

One of the advantages of seminar selling - and building your own personal brand as an expert at what you do, is that if you do it well enough, the press may take an interest in you. It's been my personal experience that seminars can go a long way towards reinforcing this expertise.

In fact, if you structure your event or seminar in a way that makes it different and unique from the way other people present a seminar, you may be able to get local or even national press coverage for your seminar program.

How can you do this? Simply spend some time thinking about how you could position your seminar and do things a *bit differently* than everyone else in the business. Then position this different approach in a way that makes it newsworthy.

Here is a quick example (Note: these are for illustrative and educational purposes only) .

THE WALL STREET JOURNAL

© *1993 Dow Jones & Company, Inc. All Rights Reserved.*

EASTERN EDITION — TUESDAY, APRIL 27, 1993 — CHICOPEE, MASSACHUSETTS

Bosses Will Do Almost Anything To Light Fires Under Salespeople

By JOSEPH PEREIRA
Staff Reporter of THE WALL STREET JOURNAL

Is your sales staff suffering from burn-out? Or lacking sizzle? Don't rake them over the coals; take them to the coals.

Fire walking — the ancient ritual of treading barefoot over a bed of red-hot embers — is catching on in sales-training programs.

A number of companies, including Digital Equipment Corp. and Metropolitan Life Insurance Co., are trying the mind-over-matter exercise, hoping to fire up their staffs. Salespeople at the Colombo Frozen Yogurt division of Bongrain North America recently walked on fire during a seminar in Danvers, Mass. The company called the session "a fabulous crescendo point for our national sales meeting."

Scott Magnacca, a Boston investment consultant and self-improvement guru who conducted the fire walk for the Andover, Mass., concern, says "a few quick steps over 1,200-degree coals will result in quantum leaps in sales performance."

Though the trek over 14 feet of glowing coals was optional, about 100 of 120 Colombo employees attempted it. Tunes like "Hot, Hot, Hot" and "The Heat Is On" blared in the background. Mr. Magnacca, in a raspy Joe Pesci voice, barked such encouragements as: "Cold calling is going to be a piece of cake after you do this."

Some participants prefer to tiptoe across. Zone manager Richard Monsees says he "high stepped it as if charging into the end zone." One saleswoman got a hotfoot when the polish on her toenails caught fire, but water quickly extinguished the flames.

Fire walking doesn't work only for salespeople. In a letter to Mr. Magnacca, Dina Pandya, assistant director of alumni relations for Babson College, says fire walking "helped me accomplish my goal of reconnecting alumni with Babson and making alumni feel good about Babson."

Mr. Magnacca says there is no real secret to fire walking. (Fakirs have occasionally confided that wet grass on both ends of the coal pit are a big help).

"My only advice," offers Mr. Magnacca, "is that after you take the first step, keep walking." First-aid kits and firemen are on hand at most of his fire walks.

Mr. Magnacca, who is writing a book titled, "Relationship Based Selling," devotes most of one chapter to fire walking. "It will help you overcome fear and procrastination," he says, "In fact, it will help you do anything short of walking on water."

The Boston Globe

SEPTEMBER 26, 1993

By Madeline Drexler

Debbie Drechsler

A BLAZING FIRE CAN MAKE A person downright reflective, especially if she's planning to walk across it. As orange flames leap skyward, and ashes drift over glowing embers, more than 60 of us gathered in the parking lot of a suburban Days Inn motel are being exhorted to do just that. "Watch your fear go up in smoke," says our guide for the evening, Scott Magnacca, a young businessman in a conservative, well-cut suit. With the aplomb of a TV game-show host, he assures us that over the next couple of hours, we can learn how to transform our mental state from fear and resignation to confidence and creativity.

But would we really walk on fire? "Yes! Yes! Yes!" we are instructed to shout, eyes closed, as two video cameras circle us. We march back to the motel, past a smiling assistant who keeps saying "Psyched?" as we file inside.

Thumping rock songs erupt every time our group is shouting or laughing. It's all part of "Unlimited Sales Power," a seminar presented by Peak Performance Development Inc., of Natick. The firm is run by Magnacca, 28, and his brother Mark, 24, both enthusiastic devotees of the mind-body connection. The power of positive belief, they say, has not only improved their health and personal lives but has also raised their corporate investment portfolio to more than $8 million, from $10,000.

Their chief commodity? Fire walking, a New Age formula for catalyzing courage and self-esteem. The idea is that if you can bring yourself to traipse across burning coals, every subsequent challenge looks piddling

Fire, walk with me

The idea behind fire walking is that if you can traipse across burning coals, subsequent challenges pale in comparison

in comparison. Veteran fire walkers also contend that their success proves that the mind can alter the body's normal perceptions and reactions to pain and can hasten healing. Skeptics question whether the coals are really all that hot; some wonder if the wet sod at each end of the fire and the cold podiatric hosing after the walk prevent the heat from searing the skin.

But the Magnacca brothers are convinced that upbeat thoughts trigger biochemical reactions that contain the damage. "If, by the end of the seminar, people still have a negative attitude, we say, 'Don't walk,' because you absolutely will burn," Scott asserts. What's missing, of course, is a control sample. Why not march cynics and scaredy-cats over the 6-foot-long bed of embers, just to compare their soles with those of true believers?

Most of the participants on this night are young (20s and 30s), gung-

ho, and apparently junior employees of large corporations, such as Fidelity Investments and The Putnam Companies, which often pay for their sessions. (The cost runs from $79 to $99 per person.) They have come to rev up their job commitment, to surmount their fears, or simply to satisfy their curiosity.

Over the next two hours, the seminar distills much of the shared wisdom of personal-growth movements, cognitive and behavioral therapy, creativity research, and common sense. Rapid-fire enlightenment comes in a series of lists: The Four Keys to Personal Power. The Six Beliefs of Success. The Three Components of Influence. The Four-Step Process for Mastering Fear. It sounds like a Chinese menu. Where were the Five Happinesses?

Yet the messages do have an invigorating effect. We learn that it's im-

portant to draw lessons from both achievement and failure, to conjure the details of a successful result, and to make a public commitment to our goals. We watch Harrison Ford leap off a cliff in a scene from *Indiana Jones and the Temple of Doom*. We break through emotional boundaries by splitting pine boards with the palm our hands and massaging the backs of strangers.

Finally, it's time to walk our talk. But there is one hitch. During our spirited lessons indoors, lightning storms have passed through the area drenching our coals while igniting fires in three nearby suburbs. By the time we tramp out, our hardwood inferno is a smoldering pile of damp charcoal, with a few glowing coals. The Magnaccas forge on. "Change your state! Change your state!" they chant. We line up in bare feet, as the halogen lights of those same two video cameras snap on at the end of the run way. One by one, we parade across. Some scamper. Some march. Some stride meditatively. Many people pump their arms in celebration afterwards. Out of habit, or duty, the crowd cheers wildly.

Did it hurt? The coals didn't even sting. When I bend over to touch them afterward, they feel like warm dinner rolls. Had I been spiritually energized, or taken in?

For most, it didn't matter. "Walking back, there was definitely an elation," says Betty, who runs a picture-framing shop. Fire walking "really is representative of life," she says. "The things you think will be big problems end up not being problems."

And a good sales pitch doesn't hurt either. ▢

Once you are perceived as an expert and a specialist at what you do, it's relatively easy to generate publicity for yourself. Just like building up your personal library of testimonial or recommendation letters, the most challenging part of the process is getting the *first piece* of publicity. Once you do that, just keep on going!

Now, that we have learned how to effectively position, promote and differentiate ourselves from the competition, let's switch our focus from the personal marketing and promotion side of the business to concentrating on how you can make a *personal connection* with the clients and prospects that you meet on a daily basis.

THE MAGIC OF INSTANT RAPPORT

One of the key benefits of presenting a seminar (financial or otherwise) or of creating and using your personal brochure is to showcase your skills, expertise and knowledge about the topic in a way that allows you to build trust, credibility and *rapport.*

What is rapport? A short definition of the word might be :

"A relation of mutual understanding or trust between people"

So Rapport, then, is all about trust, connection and mutual understanding between people. It is literally part of the foundation of the sales process. Developing rapport with prospects doesn't have to take weeks, months or years, it can happen very quickly, almost instantly if you know the right steps to take.

We're going to learn more about the topic of rapport in the next few pages, but before we do, I'd like to discuss it in the context of how you can create rapport with potential clients (i.e. prospects) before you even meet them in person. If we look to the military for a relevant example, rapport is like having accurate, real time intelligence on where the enemy is, what they are thinking and what they are likely to do next. It's an invaluable advantage if you can get it. This doesn't happen as frequently as one would like for the military, but in the sales context, the ability to quickly create rapport with prospects and clients is something that you can easily and almost effortlessly accomplish – if you know how.

One of the best ways to create rapport before you even meet a prospect face- to face is to do a bit of fact-finding or intelligence gathering in the Library or on the Internet *before* your appointment. This doesn't work all of the time, but it does work more often than you might expect.

Let me give you an example.

A number of years ago my brother and I were referred to an executive at a local technology company by a current client. An existing client of ours told us that the executive was interested in discussing retirement planning. We had his phone number and name and not much else. Rather than just calling him and "winging it" to see if we could book an appointment, we decided to do some digging before we tried for an appointment. Here is what we did.

We went to the Babson College Library in Wellesley, Massachusetts and looked for newspaper or magazine articles on him. We also did a computer search for his name. From this information, we learned where he lived (we already knew where he worked) It was in an affluent community. We also noticed that there were several other phone numbers listed for his address. From the names we assumed that they were his children (probably teenagers)

We also did a search with his name on several different library search engines and discovered that this executive had spoken at several high profile technology conferences in the last year. We were able to download and read the speeches that he gave.

We also called the company and we were able to get a description of his title, department and exactly what he did at work.

When I made the call to him to book an appointment, I mentioned that his friend had asked us to give him a call. I gave him my role statement and then asked him a few open-ended questions to get him talking a bit. One of the questions I asked was "Can you tell me a little bit about what you might want to accomplish for yourself or your family as a result of a planning consultation?" He then talked about how he had two daughters that were going to be in college in a few years and he expressed a need to save more money for them (so my guess was right, he did have two teenage children) He talked about the need to accumulate more assets for retirement and expressed the desire to have someone help him make informed decisions with his money. I told him that we could help him meet the specific goals he outlined and then I shared my personal biography and credentials with him over the phone and offered to mail my personal biography to him.

I shared my belief with him that investing successfully was a team sport, and just like at his company where there are teams of individuals that work together to support common goals, the same holds true for investing. I told him that my role was similar to that of a department head (this is what he did for a job) and that my job involved understanding my clients key financial goals and objectives and then pulling together the right people and resources to help get the job done the right way. I told him that like any good manager, I don't do all the work and have all the answers, but that I have people that I work with that do.

He was impressed with this description and booked the appointment with us. Ultimately, he became one of our best clients and most valued referral sources. The fact is, I didn't need to use *all* of the information that I gathered, but I was glad I had it. I had uncovered a lot of information on this person that I could use *as necessary* - either to book the appointment, or to use during the first appointment to help me communicate the fact that "I understood him" that "I understood his needs, lifestyle and goals" and that "I had worked with people like him in the past" Because of the information I gathered on him, his speeches, lifestyle and position I had a tremendous amount of confidence when I called him and met him in person. *I did my homework before the first call and before the first appointment and it paid off.* You can do the same.

Here is the key thing to remember:

People like people that are like themselves.

The more you share in common with someone the more of a connection you will have. Common sports teams (baseball, football, soccer), common work (knowledge of the industry that the prospect works in) common hobbies (Golf, tennis etc.)

The more you know about someone and their likes and dislikes and their beliefs and values, the more effective you will be at quickly "connecting" with them and building a relationship.

The bottom line is, if you're going to have an impact that's long term, not short term, people have got to feel that you care and that you have their best interests in mind. You need to be sincere and really mean it. People need to feel that you are willing to take the time to get to know them and their goals and dreams. In short, *people have to feel that you are like them. You've got to make that connection.* So how do you create rapport above and beyond the basic fact finding and intelligence gathering that I just discussed?

One way to do it is to talk about something where there is a *mutual interest.*

Isn't that what you've always done when speaking to customers and prospects?

The difference here is talking about areas of common interest in a *planned fashion,* rather than just by accident or coincidence. Some people would argue that this is "manipulation." I would disagree and propose to you that if you sincerely care about and are interested in the person that you are interacting with, and you really believe your product and services meets the needs and wants of the customer and the only thing holding them back is fear, then it's your job to try to connect with this person emotionally so that you can meet their needs.

Remember, it's your job to help the customer or prospect overcome the natural hesitancy that often comes up during the selling process. One of the ways you can help the customer overcome any potential fear of buying is to do a good job up front fact-finding, asking lots of questions and building trust and rapport.

Another way you can create rapport with someone is simply by ***giving him or her a small gift.*** Instantly, you'll have rapport by inducing "reciprocation".

The gift doesn't have to be something big or expensive. You could:

- Give them a coffee mug with your firm's logo on it.
- Offer to wave an account set up fee.
- Give them a free stock trade.
- Give them a gift of knowledge.
- Help them learn how to access your companies Internet web site and use the tools and features on the site.

The size or value of the gift does not matter; it's truly the thought and extra effort that counts here. Think about what happens when someone that you have just met gives you an unexpected gift or does a favor for you. Immediately you feel indebted to somehow return the favor. That's what reciprocity is all about.

Another way to create rapport is to ***ask a customer or prospect questions about some of the deep needs, wants or lifestyle goals*** that they may have.

I did this with the "prospect" in the earlier example. You could ask about:

- What they do for a living.
- What their vision of an ideal retirement would look like.
- What type of relationship they are looking for with a financial professional.

All of these questions will cause the prospect to search the various 'bar codes' in their head and think about the answer to your question. This questioning process will also demonstrate that you are interested in them and their dreams and goals. It will communicate the message that you are a true sales professional rather than a "product pusher" or "transaction orientated" salesperson.

Asking relevant questions also provides you the opportunity to find out what's really going on in this person's head - and what their *real motivations* are. Questions will help you find out their deeply held beliefs. Once you know what a person's beliefs are and how they make decisions, all you have to do is align with those beliefs, and show them how buying your product or service is consistent with those beliefs. That's all selling really is all about isn't it?

Transference of conviction and belief from you to your customer.

Good questions can also help you do things like test closing and questions can 'take pressure off' by giving you time to think during the sales presentation.

In fact, if you ask good questions, you don't have to carry all the pressure of the presentation, you can buy some time to think about your next step. You're getting the customer involved with you and sharing the burden of the conversation and sales process. Also, as I said earlier, asking questions shows that you really care about what this person is thinking. It builds more rapport and it induces reciprocation. So fact-finding questions can actually put people in a positive emotional state, since the questions you ask (if they are the right ones) may get the prospect to think about the things that they want and desire most. They can also help the prospect think about and focus on positive experiences from their past. Questions can even destroy and overcome objections and questions can ferret out hidden objections in advance. You should become skilled in not only developing rapport, but also in doing great fact-finding and asking excellent questions that lead people into emotional states where they are more receptive, less on guard and more open to wanting to buy what you have to offer.

Another way to build rapport for you is to *give the customer a referral.*

A few years back, I remember meeting a prospect in a local investor center for an appointment. As we went through the fact-finding process, I discovered that this individual had just started his own law firm in the Worcester, Massachusetts's area after working for a big law firm in Boston for 15 years. As it turned out, someone in my family was looking for estate planning help at the time and I asked this customer if he would accept a call from a potential client. Since he was just starting his business, he readily agreed. As it turned out, I made the referral and a few months later my family member did an estate plan with him. Here is the real kicker though. This prospect was so impressed that I took the time to get to know him and his needs, that *right after I offered* to make the referral he agreed to transfer over his $3 Million dollar rollover account to my firm. *Just the offer of the referral induced a strong level of reciprocity.* The fact that my family member followed up and actually did business with him months later was an added bonus. Now this customer is a client for life.

That's what relationship based selling is all about. It's about spending the time, energy and effort that most salespeople won't spend, to get to know your ideal prospects and their needs, wants, goals and dreams so well that you build a strong personal relationship with them. The strong relationship almost always results in more sales opportunities and often; it results in developing a "client for life."

Another way to create rapport is to *tell somebody a story.*

We'll talk much more about this later in the book. You may not realize it but you can get "instant" rapport with a customer by telling them a story about a client of yours who is *just like them.* Maybe you can tell them a story about someone you have worked with in the past who was of similar age to the prospect in front of you, who has a similar asset level, who has similar goals, wants and needs. By telling your prospect a story about *this other customer*, their needs, wants and concerns and then HOW YOU HELPED THIS CUSTOMER create an income plan, meet their investment needs, or overcome a particular challenge, you will almost instantly be able to very powerfully and unconsciously communicate the message to the prospect in front of you that *"I can help you"; "I am experienced and competent"* and *"I have worked successfully with people like you many times before."* Story's are one of the most powerful persuasion and rapport building tools that the human race has in its possession. And it's easy to learn how to tell stories that will support and strengthen your ability to connect with, communicate with and ultimately sell to customers and prospects. We'll learn more about this later in the book.

Another way to create rapport is *give a prospect or client a sample* of something.

If you are selling something intangible like financial services, give the customer a research report that they would be normally charged for, for free. If you are selling them an annuity or life insurance policy, tell them about the free look provision and let them know why *this is an advantage* to them as a consumer rather that letting it appear as a negative. The possibilities here are limitless.

Another way to create rapport is to give your customer or prospect a *sincere compliment.*

Review their investment portfolio and tell them all the things that they have done right FIRST. Congratulate them on good investment decisions they have made in the past. Then later you can talk to them about what they can do differently or better going forward *with your help.* Most people in life are starved for positive reinforcement and rarely get sincere compliments. In your personal and professional life, you should strive to give well-deserved, sincere complements. They are worth their weight in gold.

Another way to build rapport with prospects and customers is to give them *good service,* even before they become a client.

Show them how good you are right up front. If they ask for you to follow up and provide them with information, follow through promptly and do it. If they want an old account statement, find it for them and give it to them. If they want more information on a product or service than your product brochure can provide, get it for them. ***Providing great service is a powerful and easy way to build rapport.***

And finally, if you just ***listen to people carefully and take notes,*** you cannot believe the amount of rapport that you can generate just by paying attention, listening and taking notes.

Imagine for a moment you're sick, and you go to your doctor.

My wife, who is also a Doctor, is amazed and surprised by some of the people in her profession who seem to treat patients like they are working on an assembly line rather than being someone's father, mother, brother or sister. In some medical offices, each appointment is strictly limited to 10 or at most 15 minutes and there is no time for idle chitchat. It's strictly business.

Imagine you walk in your doctor's office to address a recurring pain that you have had for several weeks that is getting worse. Then imagine what would happen if about a minute after the doctor walks in the door and greets you, she says "You don't need to tell me anymore, I have a prescription that I think will help you. It's a powerful new drug that will numb you up from head to toe."

The reality is that you can't do an accurate diagnosis in a few seconds-you need to do some fact finding first. Chances are, this doctor would lose all their credibility with you immediately and it's likely that you would never go back.

The same thing happens in sales when you rush to sell a product before you have done appropriate fact finding and listened carefully to the prospect in front of you.

There are many people who used to be traditional stockbrokers or insurance agents who just changed the title on their business cards to "financial advisor"; "financial consultant" or "financial planning representative" without making any change in the way they communicate with clients.

Changing your business card by itself won't change anything. As an advisor and professional salesperson, not only do you need to listen to the words people use, you need to listen to what they are really saying. Sometimes what they don't say is as instructive as what they do say. The tonality and body language prospects use can also speak volumes.

GAINING AGREEMENT WITHOUT CONFLICT

If you've really been listening to your clients, one of the things you may have noticed is how offensive and caustic the word "but" can be in a conversation – regardless of whether you use it or when a prospect uses it. A prospect might say "I like your product BUT the competition..." or " I'd like to work with your firm BUT my company has an existing relationship with..." When they say things like this it probably raises your level of frustration a notch because it seems like the prospect has not heard what you have been saying to them.

On the other hand, many relationships get off to a bad start because the advisor unwittingly destroys rapport by saying "but" instead of "and."

This might sound like a minor issue, however, it can be very significant, especially in a sales situation.

When you say to somebody, "I agree with you, but this is what I think we should do," you have, in effect, just negated what they just said. This instinctively (and unconsciously) offends people. They will start to dislike you and they won't know why. If you don't believe me, try using but with your boss or spouse in all discussions just for one day. This little word is usually said with only the best of intentions, but nevertheless it causes a communication gap. Notice the difference by changing the phrase and saying, "I agree with you, **and** what I suggest is . . ."

Other ways you can do the same thing and avoid the word "but" is to say "I appreciate that AND..." or " I respect that AND...."

By using this simple strategy, you can still make your point without offending the listener, whether it is your client, boss, spouse, etc. This is a simple and effective linguistic tool for your sales toolbox.

Now try out using "and" instead of the word "but" with your spouse, a friend or a client and see for yourself how well it works.

Now you are prepared for flight and ready for taxi and takeoff.

Get ready to go through your last pre-flight checklist, to power up your engines and to start your roll down the runway for your destination.

TAKEAWAY LESSONS

- Persuasion is all about getting your prospects to associate and link their most desired emotional states to your product and service
- Remember the Ned Ryerson character from the movie "Groundhog Day?" Ned had no role statement, no personal biography, conducted no fact-finding and jumped right into trying to sell a product. How successful was he? What can we learn from his 'sales technique' regarding what NOT to do?
- Prospects are constantly weighing their options during your sales presentation. At the beginning of the sales process, there is usually a lot of 'weight' on the 'avoid buying' side of the scale or seesaw. Through effective profiling and fact finding combined with the usage of your role statement and personal biography, you can move the weight over to the 'emotional reasons to buy now' and 'logical reasons to buy now' side of the see-saw.
- Database marketing techniques can be essential for growing and building your business. Understanding the "80-20" rule and who your top customers are can help you focus and direct your marketing efforts for maximum impact.
- Celebrity endorsements, client testimonials and seminar selling can all help you more effectively communicate with prospects, reduce the 'risk' in the buying process and help to differentiate you from the competition.

- Rapport is the foundation of the sales process. Without rapport, it's nearly impossible to make a sale. There are a number of powerful, effective and very subtle techniques that you can use and apply to almost instantly create rapport and a strong feeling of connection between you and your prospect.
- Gaining agreement without conflict. Do you remember what the 'caustic' work is in sales presentations? Do you remember how to still express your opinions without offending the prospect?

KNOWLEDGE APPLICATION QUESTIONS

1. What are the key components of your personal biography?
2. Can the questions you ask a prospect change what they are focusing on and how they feel?
3. Why is fact-finding and profiling so important to the sales process?
4. Why are testimonials so powerful and effective?
5. Can you name at least 6 ways that you can rapidly create rapport with your prospects?

QUICK QUIZ- RAPPORT

1. One of the ways you can create rapport with customers is to G_____ them a G_____.
2. Another way to create rapport is to ask them questions about their N_____or W_____
3. Another way to create rapport is to tell a S_____.
4. Another way is to give the prospect a S_____.
5. Another way is to give them a S_____ C_____.
6. Another way is to give them G_____ S_____.
7. Another way is to simply L_____ I_____ and take notes.

QUICK QUIZ ANSWERS:

- One of the ways you can create rapport with customers is to GIVE them a GIFT.

- Another way to create rapport is to ask them questions about their NEEDS or WANTS

- Another way to create rapport is to tell a STORY.

- Another way is to give the prospect a SAMPLE

- Another way is to give them a SINCERE COMPLIMENT

- Another way is to give them GOOD SERVICE

- *Another way is to simply LISTEN INTENTLY and take notes

CHAPTER 6
Winning Sales Tactics During the Appointment

"Air to Air combat missions are incredibly complex and demanding both mentally and physically. An aviator needs to be able to keep track of and react to dozens of critical variables and pieces of information that can change on a split second basis. It is where the art and science of air combat meet and are put into practice"

TOP GUN Pilot
Call Sign "THUMPER"

What's ahead in this chapter:

To recap, so far in this book here are just a few of the things we've learned so far:

- *Prospects buy YOU first*
- *There are natural laws that govern the sales process, just like there are natural laws that govern flight.*
- *You need to think of ways to increase the perceived 'value added' that you bring to the sales process.*
- *Becoming a retirement income planning expert can give you and your practice a big edge over the competition*

- *Your associations direct how you feel, react and respond to events that happen in your life. You can easily change the associations you have if they do not support you in reaching your goals*
- *Most good advertising is designed to change and to create positive, favorable impressions of products and services*
- *Your beliefs and values shape who you are today and who you will become in the future. You can change the beliefs and values you have if they do not support you.*
- *Developing your personal brand by developing and using your role statement and personal biography are critical to your future sales success*
- *Positioning is focused on shaping customers perceptions so that you and your product and service are perceived in the mind of the customer in the most favorable light.*
- *People buy primarily for emotional reasons and they often justify their purchase decision with logic*
- *The proper use of testimonials, letters of reference, seminar selling and publicity can supercharge your sales efforts.*

We've covered a lot of ground so far, and we are closing in on the target and getting closer to the end of the sales process, but we are still not yet at the point where we can drop our bombs, close the sale and ask for the order.

In this chapter you will learn about the next logical step you need to take to pull everything together in a way that enables you to easily, effectively and powerfully communicate the value of what you do to the prospect sitting in front of you.

The way we will do this is by learning about the magic of "story-selling" and "sales scripting." In the coming pages we will learn how you can improve your persuasive ability by building up your own personal library of sales stories to add emotional punch and impact to your sales presentations. In this chapter I'll get you started building your library with a few powerful sales stories that I have heard top performers use with clients and prospects in recent years.

Imagine for a moment that you are a TOP GUN pilot and you are 50 miles from your target, flying over a long expanse of lifeless desert. You mission is to drop a series of 500 pound bombs on an airfield hanger and return safely back to base. Suddenly a series of blips appear on your radar screen and the AWACS plane that is supporting your mission identifies them as a flight of four MIG-29 'Fulcrum' Fighters. Your realize from your training and experience that these fighters are among the most sophisticated fighter aircraft in the Russian Air Force inventory and that the fighters are comparable to the American F-16 and F/A-18.

You realize that you will need to 'fight it out' with these aircraft in order for you to reach your destination, drop your bombs and complete your mission. You prepare yourself and your aircraft for a life or death air-to air battle. This is where all of the skills you have acquired and all of the training you have been through will pay off for you where it matters most.

The face-to-face sales process is in many aspects very similar to the 'High G Force' aerobatic flying and abrupt maneuvering for position that take place in a classic 'dogfight' between fighter aircraft. As they streak through the sky, each aircraft and pilot struggles to get in the most optimal position to maximize it's strengths, take advantage of an enemy's weakness and to fire weapons at the adversary. This 'dance in the sky' can last for seconds, for minutes- or even for a half hour or more.

In much the same way the verbal and non-verbal interaction and 'give and take' that takes place between a salesperson and a prospect mirrors a dogfight- but without the deadly consequences.

Much like technology, training and pilot skill and technique can make the difference between life and death in an aerial dogfight, the sales scripting and story-selling information that we will discuss in this chapter can make both phone or the face-to-face sales process much smoother, more natural, and less stressful. Ultimately will help you make more of an immediate impact on the prospect or client in front of you. If you use these tools correctly, Story-selling and scripting can be your 'secret weapons' for improving the odds and ultimately winning more often in face-to face sales situations.

THE MAGIC OF STORY-SELLING

Throughout history, stories and metaphors have been a powerful way of informing and communicating ideas to people. Storytelling and story selling isn't anything new. It's a skill that business and political leaders throughout the centuries have learned to use and master as a tool of persuasion. When you get good at this skill, you will be able to do it automatically and effortlessly without thinking about it, just like you drive a car.

Just like long ago you learned the alphabet and learned the letter A and B and C and then you learned how to differentiate one letter from another. You learned to recognize the small differences between the letter "O" and the letter "Q" for example. Then as your learning progressed, you discovered how to put the letters together into words and sentences that create meaning. Now you can speak complex sentences and thoughts without thinking about it- *it just happens unconsciously and automatically.*

As you begin to build *your own* personal library of sales stories based on your own personal experiences with real clients, over time, you will quickly acquire the skills you need. Just like a fighter pilot, this skill is developed over time as a result of repeated training and practice. In a moment I will give you an outline of what types of sales stories work best and how and when to best use them. This is just the beginning however. You will need to mine your past history and your past experiences with you clients to come up with real stories and situations that work for you. Then you can add them to your sales library.

As you think about what you have read in this book up to this point, I would bet that most of what you remember are the stories, analogies and metaphors that I have used to make a point. That isn't surprising. A metaphor gives the listener the ability to carry an existing understanding of something beyond its original context and into a new one. Selling via metaphor, analogy or by telling a story is something that many salespeople do at some point in their career- although usually this happens by accident when they are at an impasse in a sales presentation and are struggling to make a prospect understand the value of the product or service they are presenting. **The real magic of story selling occurs when you tell stories in a planned, organized fashion**. For example, lets suppose you were trying to explain something complex like how electricity flows through a circuit to a non-engineer. You might say something like: Imagine you go outside to water your lawn. As you turn on the hose it fills up with water. That water pressure is released when you turn on the sprinkler. The movement of the water through the hose is the same as voltage. Resistance in a circuit is the same as having something in the hose that restricts the flow of water. If the hose is on and the sprinkler is shut off while the hose is in the sun and the hose bursts due to the heat and pressure that's like blowing a fuse.

The reasons why selling via story and metaphor is so powerful and effective is because with story selling you are referencing an experience that the prospect has already experienced in their life and comparing it to something that is new and unfamiliar to them – i.e. you personally and/ or your product or service. Your goal with story selling is to help "the light bulb go on" and in it's most basic format, your goal is to help your customer understand the value of what you are offering by comparing it to something that is already familiar and known to them.

When you tell a good story, the message and the emotional impact of the story can stay with the listener for days, weeks and even years. Good stories allow people to understand, emotionally experience and feel the impact - and the message that you are communicating - far after you have physically left the appointment.

It's a fact that a good story can help to reinforce and continue the selling process long after you are gone. At it's most basic level, one only has to look to Christianity and many of the other great religions of the world to see the impact that 'the message' has had throughout the ages – And remember, this message has been primarily communicated for thousands of years in the form of stories. Without delving into religion too deeply, it has been widely acknowledged that one of Jesus' many strengths was that he was able to communicate complex ideas to the 'common man' in language that *almost anyone* would understand and could *personally relate to.*

The way he did this was not by telling people what to do, but rather, by telling them stories and providing examples from everyday life that allowed each listener to *pull the appropriate message* from the story presented.

Jesus told stories about farming, harvesting, animals, war and fighting, jealousy, ethics and a wide variety of topics and human frailties that common people of the day all had personal experience with and could relate to and understand.

And each story had a powerful lesson that people could walk away with. The fact that these stories and lessons have lasted for thousands of years is a testament to the message, the messenger and the way on which the message was often delivered (via story.)

So as you can see, when you learn how to tell good stories that have a specific purpose, a key message and emotional impact, you will be in very good company.

For our purposes here, I'd like to define story selling as the process of making the UNKNOWN, KNOWN by discussing something that is FAMILIAR.

Let me give you a quick, simple example.

Years ago I became very good at selling fixed deferred annuities to customers. Most of the people that buy fixed deferred annuities are older clients that are either approaching retirement or near retirement. Nearly all of these people also have experience investing in bank certificates of deposit (CD's). They are familiar with CD's, but often unfamiliar with how a fixed annuity works. Part of the sales process that I (and many others) have used with great success for years was to take something that is UNKNOWN (the fixed annuity) and make it KNOWN (understood) by talking about something that is FAMILIAR to the customer (i.e. a Bank CD)

I would explain to customers that a fixed annuity is very much like a bank certificate of deposit. I would ask the client why they had bought CD's the past and they would say something like "safety and protection of principal" Then I would show them how a fixed annuity could provide the very same safety and protection of principal with the *added benefits* of tax deferral and the ability to create a guaranteed lifetime income stream at some future date. In almost every case, the light bulb would go on and the client would quickly understand the basics of why a fixed annuity might work for them. Here is the interesting thing. A good, motivational sales story does not need to be long or complicated. Some stories can be delivered in 30-60 seconds while others may take several minutes or more.

Often, after delivering my "CD vs. Annuity" story to customers I would test whether or not the information actually "sunk in" by asking the customer to *explain back to me* how a fixed annuity worked by using the CD analogy. If they could communicate it back to me in a way that showed that they understood the differences and advantages of the annuity (which they were almost always able to do) then I had accomplished two things. **First**, now I knew that the customer or prospect now understand the concept I was trying to get across and they actually 'got it.' **Second**, by having the prospect repeat the story and the benefits of the fixed annuity back to me, the prospect was actually beginning the process of "selling themselves" on my product. When you can get a prospect or client to *repeat the story or example back to you* in a way that illustrates that they understand the message, then they almost sell themselves. Your just there to guide them. This is a lot easier than trying to hit them over the head with a laundry list of features and benefits. Try it. It's almost magical - and quite easy.

Story selling is all about connecting with people emotionally—not just logically. It's a natural extension from the fact-finding questions that we learned in the last chapter. Once you know about a prospects personal history, beliefs and values, the next step is to be able to relate the product or service you are promoting to something that is already KNOWN (or Familiar) to the customer in front of you in order to advance the sales process.

Good story selling, whether you are 5 years old or 50 has a number of common themes. Most effective stories are about people experiencing ordinary every day life, confronting challenges and problems, making decisions and overcoming adversity and becoming better people as a result. In my experience, there are **three types of stories** that you need to be able to develop and tell to your prospects in order to move the sales process forward.

I like to call these three stories:

3 POWERFUL STORIES TO BUILD TRUST AND RELATIONSHIPS

1. The "Trust Me" story
2. The "Other Customer" story
3. The "People & Products" story

We've already talked about these stories in one fashion or another earlier in the book, so I am not going to go into a lot of additional detail here. I'm going to share the structure and contents of these stories with you but you will need to do the work to create your own stories using the information below. Let me start by telling you what these three stories are and what they should be used for.

First, the "Trust Me" story is simply a story that you come up with that allows you to tell a prospect a quick story about your specific background, skills and experience in a way that puts them at ease and answers the question "Can I trust you?" and "Does this salesperson really have my best interests at heart?" In a sense, this type of story is simply a streamlined, verbal presentation of the highlights of your personal biography. You could tell the customer briefly about your background, education and experience and relate this to how you can help them accomplish their goals and objectives. It's as simple as that.

You could start a story like this by saying something like "You know Mr. X, the other day I was meeting with a new customer, just like you and they asked me to take a minute or two to tell them a bit about my background and experience and how I can help them. Would you mind if I take a moment and provide you with a quick overview?...."

The second type of story, "The Other Customer" story is simply based on you telling a story about a satisfied client that you have worked with in the past that is approximately the same age, has the same basic needs, wants, and concerns as the prospect in front of you. In the story, you could tell the customer in front of you how you were able to meet the needs and address the concerns of this 'other customer' by working with you and your company. By telling the prospect the story of how you helped this *other person*, they will start to say to themselves "If he/she helped that *other client* and that other client *was a lot like me*, maybe he/she can help me also." Telling a prospect a story of *another customer* that you have worked with successfully in the past who was of similar age and had similar concerns and who bought your product and service is a powerful way to create rapport, to "test close" and to get the prospect more comfortable with you and the buying process.

The final story, the "People and Products" story is simply a story that you develop that communicates to the prospect that your company and the relationship that the prospect has with your company will be much more than just a transactional relationship. The story should focus on the benefits of the product you offer, but more importantly, it should focus on all of the *experienced* people that the prospect will have working for her directly and indirectly as a result of the business relationship that is created. Let me give you a quick example.

At Fidelity, when talking to a prospect or customer, I would often explain to them that as a customer of the firm that in addition to working with me and meeting periodically, that the client would have dozens- and maybe hundreds- of other Fidelity employees working for them directly and indirectly. In the local investor center for example, they have access to a Retirement Consultant that is a specialist in the retirement rollover process and retirement planning. They have access to financial planning representatives that can help the customer with basic and sophisticated investment planning needs. They have access to dedicated specialist in the areas of income planning, estate planning, insurance and college planning. In addition, they have indirect access to a virtual army of portfolio managers, research analysts and experts in every facet of the investment process. All of these services and experts are available to the prospect once they become a client of the firm. Telling prospects about the 'big picture' in combination with they skills and expertise that you have as a sales professional can go a long way towards reinforcing the overall value of what you have to offer.

In modern times, successful story selling by great salespeople is used to help these salespeople quickly connect with customers and to help show them, through the example of a story, how to make effective decisions by leveraging off the past success of other people that have went down the path previously. Telling a story is like cutting a pathway with a lawnmower through a field of long heavy grass. Once you cut the path, rather than make their own path through the tall grass, others will often follow the path you created. A good story provides a pathway for you and a customer to follow as you move through the sales process. In the sales context, an effective "sales story" brings the products and services that a salesperson is selling to life—it stirs customers emotionally and gets customers to really think about the past, the present and the future consequences of making – or not making- a particular investment decision. As a result, the right story at the right time in the sales process can magically transform a challenging appointment into a rewarding one in the blink of an eye

GOOD STORIES IMPROVE YOUR ABILITY TO INFLUENCE

Good stories do four primary things that help improve communication.

1. They cause a listener **to relax.**
2. They cause a listener **to become less critical and more open minded**
3. They may *contain vivid images and potent messages* that often can make a lasting impact
4. They flow from one thought to another and have the ability to capture the *imagination* of the listener.

The obvious question then is how do you tell a great story? One simple answer: You practice – and you take time to think about, document and "mine" your own life, personal experience and memory to discover real life stories that you can tell to prospects that will facilitate the sales process and help influence them to buy.

If you think back in your own life, to the people that have influenced you most through the years—parents, grandparents, a special teacher or professor, a college roommate, or maybe even a fraternity or sorority member ...It's likely that your relationship with that person was built in some fashion around the stories of common experiences that you had together.

THE POWER OF SALES SCRIPTING

If you have been in the profession of sales for a while, you probably have some experience with the concept of sales scripting. Some veteran sales people think of sales scripting as "canned" and unprofessional. That's not the type of scripting that I will be discussing here. What we are going to discuss in a moment is not what you might traditionally think when you hear the word scripting. When I talk about scripting I'm not referring to writing down *every word* you will say and when you will say it. What I am referring to is having a good outline of the flow of <u>what</u> you will say and <u>how</u> you will say things during an appointment. You don't need to rehearse every word, but you do have to understand of the key points you want to get across in the meeting - and when to make the points- so that you can have maximum impact.

There is a tremendous power in taking the time to script in advance what you want to say, *before you say it*. Part of this power results from the ability to pre-determine how other people will react to what you say. If you know how they are likely to react, then you can lead them where you want to go in the sales process.

I remember a few years ago I went to see a popular comedian on the comedy circuit. The guy was fantastic and I was laughing for the entire two-hour presentation. I remember a few months later being on a trip to Florida and seeing an advertisement for the same comedian in a local newspaper. I decided to go to the show again since I liked it so much the first time. I was absolutely amazed that when I watched the presentation for the second time that *every word, every movement, every gesture and every audience interaction* was 100% scripted and rehearsed -- and believe it or not, it was just as funny and entertaining the second time as it was the first. The audience loved it. It was like watching a videotape recording- except it was "live".

I had a chance to talk to the comedian briefly after the show and in the course of conversation I mentioned that I had seen him a few months earlier in Boston. He smiled at me and asked what I thought of his show. I told him that I loved it (which was why I saw it twice) and that I was amazed that it was *exactly the same* show as I had seen in Boston. The comedian smiled at me, and with a wink in his eye, he said *"I've spent years perfecting my skits and my delivery so that I can do my entire routine in my sleep. I work hard to make sure that every joke and every gesture that I make has been tested and refined until it works every time. That's what people are paying me for."*

That's the power of scripting a performance. Movie Actors do it. People in the theatre do it. Musicians do it. Presidents do it. Trial lawyers do it- and many other professions where it is *critically important* to deliver the right message at the right time. With sales scripting, you find out what works, you test it and validate it to make sure it has the desired impact, and then you repeat it again and again until it loses it's effectiveness and you need to develop something new.

Think about your favorite television comedy show for a moment. The reason you enjoy it so much is that the dialog and the characters make you laugh. *What you don't see* is what goes on behind the scenes...the scriptwriting that drives the actors to say their dialog. *What you don't see* are the endless rehearsals and out takes. *What you don't see* is how many practice sessions or "takes" that it requires to get it right.

That's what scripting is all about. Even "live" TV is scripted for the most part. The possibility of a mistake or "blooper" is too great when millions of viewers are watching.

When most people watch a movie, they are not conscious of the fact that the actors are really speaking very well rehearsed lines from a written script. When done well, the words the actors use, the expressions and gestures, the music in the background and the visual imagery all combine together to make a powerful emotional impact on the viewing audience. In movies that have stood the test of time, the actors have rehearsed sufficiently so that they have made their lines their own and they are actually acting as if they were the character that they are portraying on the screen.

In much the same way, the words you choose to describe your product or service help create psychic real estate and a position for your product and services in the mind of your target audience. In addition, as you learned in the last chapter, the questions you choose to ask a client or prospect during fact-finding focuses the attention of your listener in a certain direction. Anyone in the sales profession who *doesn't* have certain questions to ask a prospect in a certain planned format, and anyone who *doesn't* have a variety of prepared, pre-planned responses to the common objections or questions that may come up is at an extreme disadvantage.

Top performers in almost every field, whether it is sales, consulting, or law, all take the time in advance to prepare the questions they will ask as well as the responses to questions from others. The reason this is so powerful is because the words we use literally affect people's perceptions and the associations they make in their minds. The words you choose help to create psychic real estate either positively or negatively.

Scripts come in many different forms. The one common feature? They work. Let's review a few of them to see just how powerful this concept is

Think about how a certain song playing on the radio can immediately put you into the state of mind you've previously associated with that song. For ages, music has been one of the most powerful mediums for creating powerful emotional states in people. Do you have a favorite song or artist that when you listen to their music you feel upbeat, energized and excited? How about songs that put you in a state of relaxation and tranquility? How about songs that can make you feel nostalgic and mellow? All of us have certain songs that are meaningful to us and have a powerful emotional impact on us. A song can often trigger an association with a memory from an event or person from the past. In a sense, a song that is meaningful to you has created a "bar code" in your head. When you hear that song, the bar code gets read by your brain and you immediately go into a certain emotional state.

For those of you that have children and have ever listened to the song "Cats in The Cradle" by Harry Chapin, you know what I mean. This song, which tells the story of a young boy growing up just like his father, can cause even the most hardened, macho listener to shed a tear.

In a sense, an emotional linkage or "anchor" is created between that experience and the song that you hear. If you hear a song-track to your favorite movie for example you may remember the imagery and feelings you felt when watching the movie. You may remember, for example, a song that was playing when you had your first kiss (which for most people was an emotional experience), you may remember a song that was playing at your wedding or at a particular intimate moment, you may remember a song that played at a high school or college graduation. When you hear that song you often instantly go back to the memory and feeling that you have stored away.

Here is the interesting thing. If you learn how to read music and spend some time practicing with your instrument you can create the same type of magic as the musical legends from history. For most popular music, the notes, chords and vocals of a song are arranged and mixed (or scripted) in such a way that they make a powerful, emotional impact on you. That's why you buy a CD or download a song on i-tunes. You like the way it makes you feel when you listen to it. If the chords were changed, if the notes were altered or if the vocals were out of tune, a song could go from a hit to a flop in no time flat. The same thing can happen with a poorly planned, unscripted sales presentation.

From now on, when you listen to your favorite songs, think of how they make you feel, and remember that a song is just a script set to music.

While I am not suggesting that you sing to your clients or prospects, I want you to be aware of how the power of scripted words and melodies in songs produce powerful emotional reactions in people. Remember, the lesson here is that your *words and the way in which you arrange and use them during an appointment can have a similarly powerful impact on your clients and prospects.*

One last example. Recently took a trip from Boston to West Palm Beach in Florida on Delta. On Delta, as well as all other airlines the FAA mandates that the cabin crew review certain safety procedures with the passengers before takeoff.

The next time you are on a plane, listen carefully for the safety instructions that the cabin crew provides over the intercom at the beginning of the flight. Each word they use has been carefully planned, researched and tested in order to communicate the desired information in a way that is the *least upsetting* to the passengers. On every flight you will hear this language *"In the unlikely event of a water landing, use your seat cushion functions as a flotation device."* Compare that with a script that says, "In the unlikely event of a fiery crash in the water miles from land, if you are lucky enough to get out of the emergency exit, you can use your seat cushion as a life preserver. Just watch out the pools of flaming jet fuel that are likely to be floating on the surface of the water"

Think of the words, pictures and feelings produced in you by these two different statements. The first one generates an image of a plane gently landing on the surface of the water and you floating away while holding on to your seat cushion. The second statement immediately conjures up fire, screaming passengers, and the mayhem associated with a plane crash. The effect of the words "water landing" versus "crash" is profound.

Choosing your words carefully can make a world of difference. The next time you fly and you hear the flight attendant making the FAA announcement, remember what you learned here about the power of scripting.

ANNUITY SCRIPTS

If you have been in the financial services industry for a while, chances are that you are familiar with annuities, how they work and how much most people get paid for selling them.

On most fixed deferred annuity sales brochures there is usually a statement that says "100% of the premium is invested and begins earning a return immediately." This *implies* to the client that nothing is deducted from the initial investment and that it is 'no-load.' As we all know, this is technically true, but isn't entirely true in it's application in the real world. Yes, it's true that if a customer writes a check for $100,000 for a fixed deferred annuity the entire $100,000 is invested for her. There is, however, usually a cost or commission that is paid to the salesperson by the insurance company for acquiring the business and facilitating the transaction. Most prospects are aware of this in the back of their mind and they are waiting for you to bring up how much it will cost them. So how might you answer the typical questions that a fixed annuity buyer might have regarding deferred annuities in a way that relieves their anxiety and places them at ease?

Three of the key questions most annuity buyers are asking themselves (and may or may not ask you to answer) are:

1. How much will this investment *cost me?*
2. How much will it *cost me* if I need to take money out?
3. How do you (the advisor/broker) *get paid* for this transaction?

There are other questions of course, like the safety of the insurance company, rate of interest and numerous others, but these are the big three.

First, to handle the "How much will it cost me" and "How do you get paid" questions in one quick example, it's helpful to ask the client if they have ever purchased an airline ticket from a travel agency in the past. You might recall that I used a different version of this story earlier. Most people have had this experience of buying a ticket from a travel agency. Then ask the client how much it cost them to have the travel agent do all the legwork for them (checking airlines for the best price, looking for hotels that meet their needs, arranging tours and special events.) The client will answer that it didn't cost them anything (or it was a small fee), it was just part of the service the travel agent provided. Once the client says this to you, you can explain an annuity investment as similar to purchasing a vacation trip from a travel agent. The travel agent (you) does all the legwork and research and the client doesn't pay a commission directly for booking the trip- the agent is paid a fee by the airline.

The same thing happens when clients buy an annuity. The person selling the annuity is typically paid a fee directly by the insurance company, just like a travel agent and it does not come directly out of the client's pocket. This example works very well because it is simple and straightforward. It also works because most advisors can sell annuities from multiple carriers, and just like a travel agent looking around for the best bargain for a customer, an advisor can do the very same thing and try to get the best possible rate and flexibility for a customer by shopping around with a number of different insurance companies to get the best deal based on the clients needs and wants. If someone is concerned about the penalty you can explain that the penalty for an early surrender is like an airline ticket change penalty.

RETIREMENT INCOME PLANNING SCRIPTS

One of the best ways I know of to introduce the concept of retirement income planning to a client and create interest for an appointment is the following.

Here is what I used to say to prospects:
> *"Do you know how so many investors that are approaching retirement are CONCERNED with running out of money and making sure that they have enough income to support their lifestyle? (the client will typically nod "yes" when you say this.) Well, with my clients, I help them develop a written detailed plan or roadmap for retirement that provides predictability of income, safety and flexibility."*

Typically, at this point the prospect would say "How do you do that?" and now you have an invitation to invite them into a personal appointment with you.

If the prospect does not respond by asking you "How do you do that" you can ask them the following question to motivate them a bit. The question is *"Do you currently have a written plan that can do that for you?"* The answer, of course is that they do not have a written plan that can do that. You could also ask as a follow up "I'm curious, what do you think might happen to your retirement if you DON'T have a written plan that guarantees you a certain level of income and growth?" These are questions that will cause the prospect to think—and they will likely be disturbed by the question and then they will want to talk to you further about what you can do for them from an income planning perspective.

5 POWERFUL SALES STORIES

THE AIRLINE STORY

If you are in the financial services business and you want to explain to your clients what you do and how you get paid, you can try this additional approach with them. It's similar to the travel agent story I shared with you earlier with a few key differences.

Here is what to do. Ask the prospect if they have ever taken a commercial airline flight for leisure or business purposes. Almost everyone has at one time or another. Then you can explain that your job is very similar to the job of an airline pilot. Airline pilots are highly trained to fly complex aircraft from destination to destination across the United States and overseas. Pilots get paid whether or not they are flying or they are on the ground. Their job is to use all their skill and experience to get passengers safely to their desired destination. Much of their job is routine, but the time when they really earn their money is when something goes wrong or when they experience rough weather and they need to take charge of the aircraft and bring it in for a safe landing. Passengers on the airlines can choose to travel in first class or coach. Both groups arrive at the desired destination at the same time, but one group (first class) pays more and gets *much better more personalized service* while the other group of passengers (coach) gets the basics and can purchase a ticket for a lot less. This could be used to illustrate the difference between how much a full service broker charges and a broker like Charles Schwab, E Trade or Fidelity. Thus, for some clients it will cost a bit more and advisors can spend more time with them and give them more attention and personalized service. For other clients the advisor can invest the client in mutual funds or similar investments and monitor the portfolio periodically and charge the client less.

This script/story does several things for you from a sales perspective. It positions you as a skilled professional- just like a seasoned, experienced airplane pilot. It let's customers know that, just like an airline pilot, you are paid well for your skills and experience-and clients are paying for the skill and knowledge you have. In essence, they are paying you to scan the sky in the investment world up ahead, to look out for opportunities, obstacles and rough weather and then to get them through the bumpy sky and safely to their destination. Finally, this story let's prospects know that you and your firm offer *differentiated service* to customers based on the relationship that *works best for them.* They can choose first class or coach service and you will help them accordingly. This story is a usually a big winner. Try it out.

THE AIRBAG STORY

Many financial advisors spend countless hours educating and re-educating clients about the benefits and virtues of diversification. They use statistics, style boxes and reams of investment data and charts to *prove* that diversification matters. Rather than going through all of these logical arguments with prospects, one simple and powerful way to explain the concept of diversification and why an investor would want to own bonds in an investment portfolio, along with stocks and cash, is to ask the customer the following question:

"Mr. Client, do you know if you have an airbag in your car?" Most cars these days have an airbag – and if by chance your client's car *does not* have one you can ask them if they know why *other* cars have airbags in them. They will nod their head. Next, ask them to tell you the purpose of having an airbag in a car. They will say something like *"..An airbag is designed to protect a driver in case they are in an accident"* Agree with their description and tell them that chances are that they will never get in a major accident where the airbag has to be deployed, but if they do, they will be glad to have one since it could save their life and the lives of the people they care

most about. *Then discuss the fact that proper diversification in an investment portfolio is just like having an airbag in a car.*

Just like an airbag in a car, in an investment portfolio, an investor's assets should be spread out across the investment categories of stocks, bonds and cash. The bonds and cash portion of the portfolio is the airbag for your portfolio. It protects you in case of a market decline or bear market. If you hit an obstacle (a rough market) the bonds in your portfolio will typically act as a buffer and they will tend to *expand* in price and *rise in value* as *interest rates and stock values* fall, minimizing your overall portfolio risk. The stock portion of your portfolio is like a sports car. This element of your portfolio is often structured for speed (or growth) and you need to balance this with another part of your portfolio that is structured for *safety and predictability*- that's the bond and cash portion of your portfolio. You need both working in tandem to ensure a safe journey. This explanation also works well when explaining why a retirement income plan needs both stocks and bonds as part of the portfolio.

This script/story communicates several important points. First, it explains that diversification is like having an air bag in your car. Almost everyone can relate to this. Second, the story communicates that although a minority of drivers will experience a serious accident in any one year, the odds are that most drivers over a 20-30 year time period are likely to have at least a few accidents and some will be serious.

The same is true regarding "Bear" markets. You don't know when they will hit, but the odds are that you will experience at least a few during your investment lifetime. If you are not properly prepared, this accident can "kill" your investment portfolio. Diversification, just like an air bag, will help protect you from these 'financial accidents' just like an airbag will help protect the driver from harm.

Third, this script can also communicate the fact that having an un-diversified portfolio with all equities in it is like having a brand new sports car with a powerful engine in it and driving it down a winding road at maximum speed (without wearing a seatbelt or having any safety devices to protect the driver.) Chances are it's only a matter of time before you skid off the road, crash and end up in the hospital – or worse. Just like an airbag is standard equipment on a car to protect the driver, It's a fact that proper diversification and holding bonds and cash in a portfolio can go a long way towards protecting you and your family from a deadly financial accident.

THE THIEF IN THE NIGHT STORY

Another story that you can use to drive home the impact of taxes in a powerful way is to tell the following story. Most people have a fear of someone breaking into their home-and this story should impact them emotionally and like the earlier story, should help to further reinforce the importance of tax-efficient investing. You can use this story to sell municipal bonds, variable annuities, fixed annuities, or tax-deferred accounts like IRA's or qualified plans. The story goes something like this.

Imagine that you are home alone in bed late at night one evening and you hear the tinkle of glass breaking and muffled footsteps downstairs. You jump out of bed and feel your pulse start to race as you feel beads of perspiration appear on your skin. You wonder of you should reach for the phone and call the police or venture downstairs yourself.

After a few moments, you don't hear any more noise. You wait a moment or two just to be sure and you call the police and slowly creep downstairs. When you get downstairs, you see your belongings strewn all about the room and you notice several valuable items are missing. When the police arrive you file a report -but you never see the missing items again.

As a result of the robbery, during the next week you decide to buy an alarm system and you get it installed. Despite having your expensive new alarm system, your often forget to turn it on each night, and exactly one year later someone breaks in your house and a theft happens again. You are robbed and several valuable items are taken. You are furious and upset and wonder what you can do to prevent it from happening again.

This type of situation is very similar to what happens to individual investors each and every year with their investment portfolio as the IRS "takes" up to one-third of their total returns each year from their taxable portfolios. This robbery is in the form of the taxes you pay on distributed capital gains and dividends from your taxable mutual funds. It happens each and every year regardless of whether you sell the fund or not

One of the ways to keep this "thief in the night" from taking part of your valuable assets is to make sure that your investments are concentrated in tax deferred or tax efficient investments. This is like building a huge stonewall around your house that helps prevent the "thief" from even getting near your house in the first place. This type of story can be used to sell variable and fixed annuities, tax efficient mutual funds, index funds and tax-managed mutual funds.

Here are the key messages that this script/story communicates.

- Most people are 'robbed' unnecessarily by taxes on their investment holdings each and every year- but they often don't know it.
- Average investors may lose up to 30% of their return in their taxable portfolios each year due to the eroding impact of current investment taxation
- I, as your advisor, can create a portfolio for you that helps protect and shelter your invested assets from current taxation. As a result, my advice will likely pay for itself many times over[4]

---

4 [4] Of course, as a financial planner, unless you are also an attorney or a CPA, you cannot provide legal or tax advice to clients. You can, however educate the customer on basic concepts and then direct them to the appropriate, licensed planning professional.

MARKET TIMING AND DIVING

This is a script/story that I heard a few years ago from one of the top advisors in the financial services industry. It's very effective at teaching clients about the importance of investing based on a plan vs. investing based on gut instinct or emotion. Here is how the story goes. Numerous research and investment studies have been done over the years that have proven beyond the shadow of a doubt that the individual investor, left to his own devices, will often buy into stocks at *high prices* and sell them at consistently *low prices*. Customers try to time the market and they often do not succeed.

Individual investors often react emotionally to the current news in the media and typically sell out of stocks right at market bottom (usually right before a big upturn in stock prices) and then these individual investors buy into stocks at the heights of the market (typically right before a market correction or downturn)

This is like a **cliff diver** jumping only when a wave crests beneath him, without realizing that the right time to actually jump off the cliff is when the *trough* of the wave passes below.

Cliff divers can provide a clue to individual investors that they can use to remind themselves about an important investment principal. First, if you are smart, you should not be jumping off a cliff -or into and out of the market anyway. Sooner or later you will end up on the rocks. However, if you insist on doing this, to be a successful cliff diver, the diver needs to

<u>over-ride</u> his natural instinct to jump off the cliff and dive when a wave is passing underneath him, *and instead jump when the trough or gap in between the waves goes underneath him.* The cliff diver needs to jump when it looks the most dangerous to do so. The reason for this? If a cliff diver jumped when the wave was cresting beneath him, by the time he actually hit the water, the crest of the wave would have passed and the water may have receded enough to expose the dangerous rocks below.

Cliff divers need to mentally train themselves to jump at the very time that all their instincts and senses tell them that they should not. It is the same with investing in the stock market. When the press, newspapers and magazines are all talking about collapsing stock prices and there is panic and "blood in the streets" the trough in the wave is passing underneath you and this might be the time to jump into the market and increase your stock exposure based on your individual risk tolerance- even though your 'gut' and your common sense would tell you not to do it. Warren Buffett, one of the most successful individual investors in modern history follows this very same investment principal. If it's good enough for him to use, then it should be good enough for the average investor.

On the flip side, when everyone is making money hand over fist in the market and the rising stock market is the main news item in the newspaper and magazines, this might be a good time to take some profits and scale back some of your equity investments.

> *"Most people get interested in stocks when everyone else is. The time to get interested in when no one else is. You can't buy what is popular and do well."*[5]
>
> **-Warren Buffett**

TAKEAWAY MESSAGES

- Story-selling is all about making the UNKNOWN, KNOWN by talking about something that is FAMILIAR
- There are three basic types of sales stories you need to be able to tell. They are the "Trust Me" story, the "Other Customer" story and the "People and Products" story.

---

5 Ann Hughey, Omaha Plain Dealer, Newsweek, April 1, 1985 p 56.

- Good sales stories do 4 key things. Do you remember what the four are? Check page 103 for a refresher.
- Sales scripting is a powerful way to shape and craft the messages you deliver to prospects so that they have maximum impact.
- The music business uses scripts. So does Hollywood. So does the President. So does every salesperson that is a true professional. Good scripts, just like good movies, don't sound 'canned' but quite to the contrary, they can produce powerful emotions in the mind of the listener.
- Do you remember the 5 Sales Stories That Top Financial Advisors all Use? If not, review this section again.

KNOWLEDGE APPLICATION

Answer the following question and complete the activities:

1. When you think back to the great political and business leaders that have influenced millions of people with their words, who come to mind? Name the top 5 communicators or persuaders from the past or present day that have impacted our society. Ask yourself; did these people utilize scripts and story selling as a key tool of influence?
2. Re-Read and practice the "Investment Scripts and "Annuity Scripts" contained in this chapter and then test them out on live prospects within the next week. You will be amazed with results
3. Do you remember the key messages of the Airline, Airbag, Reduce Taxes, Thief in The Night and Cliff Diving stories? Re-read these stories and commit to using at least 1 story each week with your prospects. As you test each story, document what works and what does not and refine each story so that it fits your specific style and your business.

Photo Courtesy of N.A.S.A.

CHAPTER 7
Retirement Income
Referrals-Your 'Force Multiplier'

"The best part of a successful mission is returning to base with no casualties and then being able to pass on real time intelligence to the mission planners and pilots that will be conducting subsequent missions. Part of my job is to make things safer for the pilots who come after me"

TOP GUN Pilot
Call Sign "VIPER"

On January 16th, 1991 at 6:38 PM Eastern Standard Time the Air War over Iraq commenced and the Gulf war began. US aircraft and commando teams attacked Iraqi positions throughout Iraq, inside of Kuwait and in and around Baghdad as hundreds of bombs and cruise missiles rained down on Iraqi military targets across the country.

In the months and weeks leading up to the war, as US and allied troops were massed in Saudi Arabia, a tremendous quantity of intelligence was gathered on the location, disposition and capabilities of enemy forces, troop concentrations and weapons depots.

The success of the early air strikes on Iraq by allied fighters and bombers set the stage for the rest of the air war -and the ground war that would follow- by providing commanders with a treasure trove of information on enemy troop concentrations, weapons systems, communications methods and tactics. This real-time intelligence was used to improve the accuracy and results of the many hundreds of subsequent missions that followed in the first weeks of the war. In the sales world, part of the way that we know that we have become successful in our mission is if prospects buy from us. This is one important measure of success.

Another way we can define 'mission success' is that if we don't get the sale the first time around, we want to make sure that we gain enough information about the prospect and his needs and wants so that we can go back to the office, debrief with a peer or manager, evaluate what we have learned and then prepare for the next follow up meeting or 'mission'. Once you have met a prospect and they are qualified and do not buy, they should go into your 'drip' marketing program where you reach out to them quarterly via email with educational ideas. In selling, just like in war, sometimes bombs miss their targets- even when you have the best technology and the most skilled pilots. When this happens, you learn from what worked -and what did not -and you try again until you succeed.

In the sales world, if you target and identify you're prospects with the right database marketing and profiling techniques then there are truly never any failed missions. You can't fail if you learn something. You will either make the sale or you will be able to gather enough information about the customer, his needs, wants and desires to make another run at the target on a subsequent appointment.

In fact, in a professional selling situation, or one that involves financial services, high priced technology items or 'big ticket' real estate purchases for example chances are very good that you will not get the sale on the first or even the second or third appointment. It will likely take many meetings and appointments for you to build the relationship and close a sale. Each meeting then is like an intelligence gathering mission where you get to learn more and more about the target so that when it comes time to let the bombs fly, you increase your chances of hitting the target.

In fact, one could also argue that once a prospect buys from you and becomes an actual customer or client, the sales process has just begun. Most transaction-orientated salespeople view the sale as the <u>end</u> of the selling process. Once they make a sale they are off to meet with another prospect, and the person who just bought from them may —or may not - see them again for weeks, months, or maybe never. The money management business is notorious for this type of short-term thinking. Often, once the manager gathers the assets they often do nothing for the customer except sending them legally required quarterly reports and expect that inertia will keep the business in place. That's a big mistake. Professional, relationship focused salespeople on the other hand, view the sale as the beginning of the process, not the end.

If you do your job well up front and focus on exceeding customer expectations you will build the relationship and create the opportunity for many additional future sales opportunities. This will also lead over time to the opportunity for 'endless referrals.'

Here's why.

Most people have heard the statement that a 'satisfied customer' is your best source of repeat business. But is this really true? The answer, of course, is YES. Once a person buys from you and has an above average experience with you and your company, often they will be happy to tell other people about it. Unfortunately, chances are that most people have such bad experiences with most average salespeople that they are used to telling friends and associates all about the 'horror stories' rather than the 'success stories.'

Despite what we many of us in sales may think, people DO like talking about what they have bought when they feel that they have made a good decision. It makes them look good and validates the above average judgment and decision making skills that they believe they have. To get people satisfied with you and your products and services is easier than you may think. All you need to do is follow through on your commitments in a timely fashion. Make sure what you promised actually happens when you promised it. Stay in contact with the customer through email, phone or face to face after they have bought. Let them know you are thinking about them and that you have their best interests in mind. Once they have received their product or have interacted with you for a period of time, ask them if they would provide you with a reference letter that you can then use as a 'client testimonial.'

If they have had a good experience with you and if you have maintained ongoing contact with them after the sale, chances are they will be glad to provide you with a reference letter.

In my twenty plus years in the sales and marketing profession, not one of the salespeople I have ever interacted with and bought something from has ever asked me to provide a reference letter for them. When I have bought boats, cars, houses, and investments both big and small, no one has ever asked me to provide a reference letter to them. And very few of them have followed up with me on an ongoing basis after the sale. Chances are, you may have experienced the same or a similar type of situation in your life as well. The reason I mention this to you is to point out the fact that almost no one asks for reference letters- ever- except the really good salespeople out there.

The top 1% of professionals that work in the sales business do this regularly. That's one of the reasons they are in the top 1%. This is exactly the same reason why you should do it. Since so few people actually do, you will immediately stand out as different and unique.

All it takes is one good customer letter to get started building up your three ring binder of 'satisfied customer' testimonials. Once you have received reference letters you can ask these very same people for the names of 2-3 friends or associates that they think may be able to benefit from the product or services that you provide. If they have already provided you with a letter of reference, it's almost unthinkable that they would refuse to give you a few names of other qualified people that you could call.

REFERRALS- YOUR 'FORCE MULTIPLIER'

In the military, a 'force multiplier' is defined as "A capability that, when added to and employed by a combat force, significantly increases the combat potential of that force and thus enhances the probability of successful mission accomplishment". The referral process can be considered a 'force multiplier' for your sales career. The simple reason for this is because existing, satisfied customers are your best source of generating 'quality leads' We've all heard the statistic that recent studies have shown that on average, customers tend that have a "bad" experience with a company or a salesperson will often tell between 8-10 friends, associates or family members about it. The flip side of this situation is that, on average, customers that have a "good" experience will often tell 5-7 people about it.

Imagine what could happen if each one of the clients that make up just the **top 20%** of your current customer base each gave you between 5-7 referrals each? You probably would sell a lot more and have to spend a lot less time, money and energy in the prospecting process.

REFERRALS AND RETIREMENT INCOME-
WHAT YOU CAN EXPECT

Here is a hidden secret about retirement income planning that many of the big financial firms don't want you to know about. If you do income planning with your clients and they like the result (which they will if you follow the simple process outlined earlier in the book), on average you will get 3-4 new referrals from each income plan you complete for an existing client. If you have 300 clients and they all need a written income plan, there is a very real possibility that creating a plan for each client will result in you seeing an additional 900-1200 clients due to the referrals you receive. Think about what would happen to your business if it were to triple in size and all of your clients looked just like your very best, most profitable clients.

At Fidelity, when we ran income-planning seminars for the general public, on average we would experience the following type of results:

- On average, the vast majority of attendees ranked the seminar good, very good or excellent. The seminar was educational in nature and did not promote any specific investment products For clients that sat through an income planning seminar between 60-80% of the clients that attended wanted a follow up appointment with a planner/advisor

- Of the clients that met with a planner/advisor, approximately 70% of them did additional business with the firm over the next 180 days

- The typical appointment cycle of two face to face appointments produced (on average)

- A Rollover of $180,000

- A Managed account of $110,000

- A Mutual fund sale of $60,000

- An Annuity sale of $120,000

- 3-4 qualified referrals of friends/co-workers that would be interested in having a plan created by the advisor/planner

Although the individual product sales are significant, pay special attention to the last point above. Three to four qualified referrals from each successful appointment. That is where the value of the relationship and loyalty really will pay off for you in the long run.

Over the years it's been estimated from various media reports that Fidelity has taken in over $15 Billion in net new assets related to retirement income planning. And this is just scratching the surface of the opportunity. *This is why income planning is so critically important to your business. People who need income planning have money, they are motivated and they need to do something now. The plan you create is the catalyst that gets the consolidation and profit engine going.*

So if everyone agrees that referrals can be a powerful way to turn new prospects into satisfied clients, why doesn't everybody do this? Everyone has heard that in order to get referrals, you need to ask for them. So why is it so hard for most people to ask? I believe there are two reasons.

First, as I just mentioned, because many sales people have such a transaction orientated mentality and methodology, they are often happy to just get out the door with a sale and a completed order blank. They worry that if they call the customer back that the customer might change their mind and cancel the sale. **So they typically never call the customer after the sale is made.** Big mistake. This lack of contact after the initial sale often becomes a self-fulfilling prophesy because it causes the customer to begin worrying about what happened to his or her money - and whether or not anyone cares about them. This doubt often creates buyers remorse and this can be toxic to the sales process. It sets the stage for the phone call you dread if you are in sales. The call that starts with "I've changed my mind…"

It's also certainly not the way to create a relationship with a new customer. Taking their money and never calling them back is generally a bad idea. Remember; be different than the army of other salespeople out there competing for sales and client dollars. If you follow up after the sale, follow through on your commitments and let the customer know that you care about them this will pay big dividends for you later on both in the area of additional business and referrals.

Second, most advisors do not have a clear script to follow that will produce the desired result of a referral. The most successful referral prospectors are those advisors who are **absolutely convinced** of the value they bring to the table.

What I have found in studying some of the best referral prospectors in the business is their excellent timing regarding asking for a referral. While there are many schools of thought on this matter, I think it is inappropriate to ask for referrals before you have done anything to prove you deserve one. That's why I recommended asking for a 'reference letter' first once you have actually demonstrated the value or what you bring to the table for the customer.

Instead, the first step I recommend in beginning your referral process is to review your existing customer database using the ideas covered in Part One of the book to determine who your best, most profitable customers are. These are the people I would begin focusing your attention on for referrals.

The reason is simple. All people are not created equal when it comes to giving referrals. There are certain people for whom giving referrals comes easily and others for whom it is very difficult.

Focus first on your clients who are enthusiastic about you and what you do.

You know who these people are.

As you know, there are some people whose personality allows them to become convinced about your skill level and competence after just one or two appointments, but such people are the exception rather than the rule. At the other end of the spectrum, there are people you can know for twenty years who trust you implicitly but will still not give you a referral. The vast majority of people fall somewhere in between.

Start by asking for referrals from the clients you know are the most supportive and enthusiastic about you, your products and your company.

Start with the easy ones and the rest will come over time.

Earlier in the book I discussed the concept of using a fish finder as a metaphor for identifying and locating your ideal prospects and customers. The first challenge fisherman face is to find a school of fish in the vast ocean. The next challenge is to get the fish interested in what you have to offer- and to find out what type of bait or lure they are biting. Fish, just like people, have preferences both for environmental conditions and food. Some fish bite best in rough water, some like smooth water. Some fish bite best in cool water, others like warmer temperatures. Some like live bait, others like lures. It's up to the fisherman to make informed decisions and to test out various bait options to see what works and what does not based on environmental conditions, intuition and experience. As I mentioned earlier, just like some fish will only feed at a certain water temperature, some people will only give you a referral when they have known you for a certain amount of time.

One of the best ways you can determine whether somebody is going to give you a referral is by asking them the following questions (My assumption here is that any client you ask these questions to has been a satisfied client of yours- at least for a few months.)

Here are the questions:

1. "Mr. Client, would you say that you are satisfied with the service and support that I have provided you so far?"
2. "Mr. Client, can you tell me what is most important to you before you decide to make a referral to your friends or family about a product or service you are satisfied with?"
3. Mr. Client, if you have made referrals to friends or family in the past about various products or services that you really valued, is this something that you tend to do regularly - or infrequently?

Depending upon how they answer these questions, you will have a tremendous insight into their 'referral temperature' and whether or not you will get a bite when you ask for a referral from them.

If they struggle as they think about the questions, it is reasonable to believe that they probably don't refer products or services they are satisfied with very often.

On the other hand, if they answer the question by saying, "I need to have some time to experience the product or service before I ever make a referral to anybody else," then you have a benchmark for understanding this person's values and beliefs regarding referrals.

You can then ask a follow-up question such as:

> "On average, how long to you have to own and experience a product before you are comfortable recommending it to others?"

And then let them answer. Some people are convinced quickly over a period of days and weeks. Others take a much longer time- sometimes months and years. Each person is different and has a different referral temperature so make sure to ask them. This way you won't ask for a referral from a client who is not ready or has not reached the correct 'referral' temperature.

Earlier in the book when we learned about the topic of letters of reference/recommendation and testimonials I shared a number of examples with you of testimonial letters that I asked satisfied clients to write on my behalf. One of the natural ways that reference/testimonial letters and referrals work hand in hand is if someone is willing to put their personal thoughts and opinions about you and the service and support your company provides down in writing (Remember the concept of **commitment** and **social proof** we learned about earlier in the book?) Then this person would also be a great candidate to ask for referrals at a later date. Often, I would be able to get a letter of reference and a referral at the same time by asking clients for a letter of reference first and then asking this simple question:

> "Mr. Client. I really appreciate the fact that you're willing to take the time to write a letter of recommendation/reference for me. Thank you. I was wondering if you could give me some advice. *If you were in my shoes, who would you recommend talking to in the future about the products and services I provide?*"

This simple referral script does several powerful things. First, it leverages off the fact that the client has agreed to write a letter of recommendation for you already. If they are willing to do this, a referral is a small matter by comparison (Remember the tool of contrast?)

Second, by asking the person for their opinion regarding who you should talk to about your products and services you are telling the client that you highly value his or her opinions. Everybody likes to be asked their opinion on something and when asked, most people will gladly provide you with 'advice' regarding whom to talk to. This is a very non-threatening approach that has no real downside.

The worst thing that can happen is you get the reference letter. The best thing you can get is the letter and a handful of qualified referrals. This is one of the key ways that I built both my investment advisory business and my sales training business into multi-million dollar firms. It works, and it will work for you as well if you use it. But don't use it too quickly. I don't want you overwhelmed with clients or extra discretionary income ☺

THE REFERRAL UMBRELLA

For those of you that are fisherman, you may be familiar with a specific type of lure called an umbrella rig. This is a lure that looks kind of like an umbrella that typically has a lure in the middle and 4 or 5 other lures with separate hooks hanging around it. This is a highly successful way to catch fish because all of these lures together in the water look like a school of baitfish to hungry bass or bluefish. It's not uncommon to hook up with 4 or 5 fish at the same time when using this lure.

The reality is that an umbrella lure is a very efficient way to fish since you typically will reel in 3, 4, or 5 fish at the same time vs. just one when you are using a traditional lure or bait with 1 hook. Some fisherman refuse to use umbrella's because they say that it makes fishing too easy and effective.

Imagine for a moment that the lure in the center is one of your satisfied clients. He or she has generated significant revenue for your practice and as you build the relationship with the client and create a high degree of client loyalty this client is likely to give you 4 or 5 referrals of new clients that look just like he does.

What is the result? Instead of one ideal and highly profitable client you now have 4 or 5 of these clients as a result of the referral process.

What is the value of that 1 initial client? It's not the initial commission or fee revenue that you derive from that one client; it's the combined revenue that you derive from that client and all of the qualified referrals that you receive from that client over time. That's called a force multiplier.

By Let me share one final story with you about referrals. Several years ago before I joined Fidelity I met an older prospect that lived near me. He was referred to me by another long time satisfied client who was an old friend of his. This prospect became a valued client and friend through the application of many of the strategies and techniques I shared with you in this book. He ended up ultimately becoming one of my best clients and a valuable referral source. He trusts me implicitly and I treat him like a member of my own family.

Recently, I decided to give him a surprise for the holidays. I knew that his wife had passed away and that he lived alone with his son. He is a multi-millionaire and is a living case study right out of the book The Millionaire Next Door. He is very frugal - and I knew that he almost never went out to eat or did anything special for himself- his idea of a night out was a visit to the local McDonalds.

As a result, I decided to buy him a holiday dinner (Turkey and all of the fixings) and personally prepare it for him and deliver it to him as a surprise. It cost me $50 and a few hours of my time. When I delivered it to him on Christmas morning he was in shock. I saw a tear in his eyes as he told me the last time he had a really good holiday meal prepared for him and his son was nearly a decade ago when his wife was still alive.

He thanked me profusely and I felt really good about doing 'something extra' for someone I had grown to care a lot about over the years. Before I left his house, my client excused himself and went into his bedroom for a few moments. When he returned and walked me to the door, he surprised me by handing me a very special gift that was both highly meaningful and quite valuable. In fact, the gift was worth many times more that the time and effort I had invested in the gift I gave him. Part of the gift he gave me was a gift of a referral to his five best friends in the world- people that had known him for the last 40 years. Each one of these friends had portfolios that were in mid seven-figure category in terms of assets. He also said he would call each of them for me and encourage them to meet with me.

This was one of the most priceless gifts he could have provided to me, and he did it because of the relationship, friendship, loyalty and trust that we had built up over time. Remember the tool of reciprocity that we discussed in the last chapter? This is a great example of what can happen when you give value first to people when they don't expect it.

What was the true value of this one client in terms of revenue to my practice? Remember the "Umbrella" concept that we just discussed? When I added up the fee income that I derived from him and the 5 referrals that he gave me the recurring revenue was approximately $50,000 per year each and every year. **Was it worth it? You tell me.**

The lesson here is simple. Build relationships. Give value first. Go the extra mile and do special things for people in a unique and different way and you will be paid back twenty-fold over time. Realize that some referrals will happen more rapidly than others. Ask for them using the simple scripts and techniques I outlined in this chapter.

But be patient.

As the old biblical saying goes, seek and you shall find, knock and the door will be opened for you.

In almost all of the stories that I have shared with you in this book, a number of the tools and techniques that I have discussed were used and applied with prospects to create and build relationships with them. Each of the tools you have learned should not be used in isolation. Think of all of the instruments that a pilot needs to pay attention to and monitor simultaneously during takeoff and flight. They don't just pay attention to the airspeed indicator. They continuously scan the instruments -and the airspace- in front of them and around them while looking at dozens of variables like speed, direction of flight, angle of climb, engine speed, rpm's, weather conditions and a host of other variables to make sure they are doing the right things to ensure a safe and eventful flight.

In much the same way, over time you will begin using many if not all of the tools and techniques I have discussed in this book on appointments-from the techniques of changing associations, unconscious influence, to shaping beliefs, values and perceptions through the use of role statements and personal biographies, to asking great fact-finding questions and using sales scripting and story-selling with clients and prospects.

TAKE AWAY LESSONS

- The most profitable way to grow your existing book of business is from referrals.
- **Ask** long term, satisfied clients for a letter of reference/recommendation first, and then follow the steps outlined in this chapter to position the referral opportunity.
- **Clients don't owe you a referral**. Don't push. Ask them the right way and make the request 'non-threatening'
- **Follow up**. Always let the person who gave you a referral know the outcome of the meeting.

PULLING IT ALL TOGETHER: MISSION DEBRIEF

"Success is all about accomplishing your
Mission and coming home safely "

TOP GUN Pilot
Call Sign "ROCKY"

What's ahead in this chapter.

So far in this book, we've covered a great deal of powerful, cutting edge information and discovered dozens of innovative sales ideas and 'best practices' that are designed to improve your sales skills and persuasive power while building, clarifying and positioning the value of your personal brand to clients and potential prospects.

In this chapter I would like to issue you your 'go orders' to take the information you have learned in the previous chapters and to **take action** with it. This book has given you the tools and skills and ideas that can help you make a quantum leap in your sales career and your overall sales effectiveness. **What you actually decide to do with the information is totally up to you.** When you put this book down, you can walk away feeling that you have learned a few good ideas and concepts - and you can continue to live your life and work at your career in the same way you have been used to. Or, alternatively, you can decide to take the information and ideas you have discovered and you can decide to put these ideas to work for you right now.

The tools you have learned in this book are powerful and effective. They are like a carpenter using the latest electric drills and saws competing against another carpenter who uses old fashioned, hand driven equipment. Both of these carpenters will get the job done- eventually. But when you hire a professional that uses electric tools, he can can speed up the construction process dramatically, he can make it more efficient and he can help both the customer and the craftsman save both time, effort and money.

Your mission is to go out and bring the knowledge, information and strategies that we have learned together to life with real people in the real world.

In the military, when the National Command Authority (Typically the President an/or The Secretary of Defense) provides the final sign off and authorization for military action, it is often informally called a "Go-order."

Consider this chapter your "Go-order" to go out in the world and create 'eye-popping' results and deep, long lasting relationships with your clients, your prospects, your co-workers, your peers and your family.

It's much easier than you might think. All it takes is a commitment to taking the first step. Once you take the first step, keep on going.

One of the first things that a student pilot learns in his first lesson in ground school is the takeoff speed of the aircraft he or she is going to be flying. This speed, which is different for every aircraft (and varies with weight of the aircraft with the air temperature, with wind conditions and with usage of wing flaps) is known as **V1 or takeoff speed**. This is the speed at which the pilot must make the "go" or "no-go" decision to continue with the takeoff or to abort.

This speed is critical because once it is passed; there is a very high probability that the pilot could not safely land the plane back on the runway in case of an engine failure or other unforeseen problem. If the pilot has a problem before reaching this speed, he should abort the takeoff.

If a problem occurs after reaching this speed, he should proceed with the takeoff.

The next critical speed is known as 'rotation speed' or VR. This is the speed at which the pilot begins to lift the nose of the plane into the air and the wheels leave the ground. Usually, under normal conditions these two speeds (V1 and VR) are reached in quick succession during takeoff (typically within a matter of 5-10 seconds or less)

On every flight you take, your pilot is faced with making the "go" or no-go" decision for takeoff. It's a decision that can have life or death consequences.

The decision you have to make right now is equally important- and the point here is simple. The information you have learned so far in this book has been designed to teach you the strategies, ideas and concepts that you need to know to successfully reach takeoff speed and then to 'rotate' your aircraft and get safely into the air so you can complete your mission.

As we have learned, each pilot goes through countless hours of academic training that cover physics, aerodynamics, weather, air-to-air combat techniques, weapons systems and dozens of other disciplines that are related to flight. They learn to do checklists and follow exacting procedures to maximize their chances for success during takeoff, flight and landing.

All of this time spent, all of this information, and all of the training they do is completely useless to them until and unless they sit in the pilot's chair, strap themselves in, go through their checklists and procedures and make the decision to head out on the runway.

Again, what you choose to do with this information is up to you.

My hope is that you will use and apply it and not just let it waste away on a bookshelf somewhere. Don't get stuck in the mindset of a student that pursues education just for the sake of gaining more knowledge. Unless you are a scientist or a professor and you get paid for accumulating knowledge and doing research, it's value to you as a salesperson is questionable.

I strongly encourage you to become a practitioner of excellence by using and applying what you have learned to improve your own life and the lives or your clients and prospects.

Lets end by quickly touching briefly on the key lessons we learned in this book and then help you analyze, apply and build upon much of what you have learned in order to create you own "syllabus" of TOP GUN sales success that you can use and apply in the coming weeks and months.

TURNING THE AFTERBURNERS ON!

The purpose of an afterburner in military fighter aircraft is to dramatically boost the speed of the aircraft for a short period of time. The afterburner is typically used when an aircraft needs to get into the air and into a fight with an enemy quickly, or conversely, it can be used after firing a missile or dropping a bomb, when the pilot wants to 'hit the gas' and get out of the area quickly.

In this book, we have learned about the key elements that go into planning and executing a successful sales mission. **First is the mission planning phase.** We covered this in the first section of the book. The pilot needs to have a keen understanding of the overall mission, it's goal and objectives and all of the elements that are required to make the mission successful. They need to know if they will need to be refueled on the mission and when and where this will take place. They need to know about other friendly aircraft that will be operating in the target area. They need to know the flight plan and routes to the target. From a sales and relationship building perspective, in this section of the book we learned about the fact that you and I are in the relationship building business not the "product" business. We learned about the history of the TOP GUN school and the physical and mental training that TOP GUN pilots are subjected to. We learned about the fact that one of the secrets of TOP GUN was the development of a comprehensive, documented syllabus of best practices that were learned and developed from interviewing the best pilots from across the fleet and then sharing this information with other pilots through the TOP GUN school. We learned about the critical role that the individual pilot and his level of skill and training play in the success of the mission and the fact that the aircraft and its weapons systems were of secondary importance. All of these concepts are directly transferable to the profession of selling. In sales, your primary mission is to build relationships with the right people and to either close the sale or to advance the sales process.

We learned about the concept of **value-added** and being **perceived as an expert**-not a transaction orientated salesperson. We learned about developing your **passion to win** and applying a **"TOP GUN" mindset** to your sales and relationship building efforts. We learned about the **power that unconscious 'associations' and 'anchors'** have over what you think, how you act and how you behave now and in the future. We learned about the **beliefs of success** and discovered how these beliefs were used and applied by **top business leaders, marketers and politicians** and countless others to shape their thoughts and actions in a way that put them on the path to success. We learned **about creating and building your personal brand** so that you can differentiate yourself and stand out from the competition. We learned that **branding and positioning** is simply good marketing and that you don't need to be a FORTUNE 500 company to apply it. We learned that **people often buy for emotional reasons and justify their buying decision with logic**. We learned how you can develop and use your own **personal role statement** and **personal biography brochure** to position you as a valued expert.

From a sales and relationship building perspective, we learned that as a salesperson, although you are the 'pilot' and get much of the glory when a sale is made (and much of the headache when it is not) that **you depend on an extended team of support personnel**, both in the field and in the home office to help you get your 'mission' accomplished. In this section of the book you learned about the power and impact of **effective database marketing** and how both you and your firm can use these database-marketing techniques to maximize the impact you have in your sales presentations by talking to the **right people with the right offer at the right time**. You learned about the **80-20 rule** and how to quickly analyze your own personal book of business **to identify and profile your most valuable and profitable clients and prospects**. You learned about the **power of 'reference letters' and client testimonials,** the impact of **seminar selling** and **publicity** and how you can utilize these tools in your own practice. You learned about the **power of rapport** and discovered **6 simple steps** you can quickly take to create almost **instant rapport** with customers and prospects and to begin the relationship building process.

In the final section of the book we discussed the various techniques that you could employ to gather information about your prospects before you arrive at the first appointment. We also discussed the critically important role that **fact-finding and asking good questions** play in both creating rapport with a prospect and gathering intelligence and information that can be used when you present alternatives, narrow choices and close the sale. We learned about the magic of **'Psychographic' customer profiling** and the **magic of sales scripting** and **how to use story-selling techniques** to present and communicate ideas to customers in a way that is both non-threatening and highly effective. We learned how to use sales scripting and story selling to present **managed accounts, mutual funds, annuities** and other investments to customers.

The final stage that we are in right now is the Mission-Debriefing phase. In this phase the **result of the mission is analyzed**, any problems and issues that developed on the mission are documented and fixed so that they don't happen again. In addition, an overall assessment is made regarding whether or not the mission was successful. Did the bombs that were dropped hit and destroy the desired target? If the mission was not successful, planning then begins for another strike at the target to finish the job and accomplish the mission.

From a sales and relationship building perspective, the results of your missions will be something that you should **document and review** after each sales interaction. A good sales manager can help you with this. It's important that you do an **appointment debriefing** soon after your appointment so that the details of the appointment are still fresh in your mind and so that you don't forget any important details. In the military, a mission debrief often takes place very soon after the pilot lands. They don't wait for a few days or for a week or two to pass before they conduct the mission debriefing. They do it immediately so that the information is fresh. You should do the same with your appointments and 'debrief' at the end of each day with your manager or a business associate. Once you apply these strategies and ideas you have learned on a series of real live appointments with real people I am confident that you will be shocked and pleasantly amazed at the results. Just like a TOP GUN pilot, once you try these techniques out, you will begin to see what specific techniques work best for you as an individual. You'll also learn what you need to spend more 'training time' on and what strategies you may want to postpone for a later time until you further improve and develop your skills.

As you probably are aware, we have covered a lot of information together in this book and by now you may feel like a novice pilot that is seated behind the controls of a sophisticated jet. In front of you are dozens and dozens of gauges, switches and dials that can tell you critically important information about the status of your aircraft and it's weapons systems.

The only way you can effectively learn to use and apply the information that these gauges are telling you is to break the learning down into manageable bite sized pieces of information so that you can learn and master each piece before moving onto the next one. Then once you learn the task in it's entirety, you will need to practice and refresh your skills on a periodic basis. That's what TOP GUN pilots do in their training.

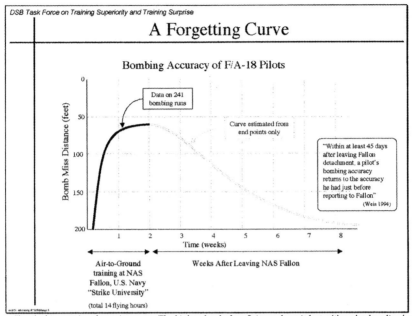

Sketched in gray is a forgetting curve. The highest level of proficiency doesn't last, although a baseline level remains. Peak performance can often be restored quickly by refresher training. Note that the time between most predeployment training and combat during that deployment exceeds the forgetting time.

In the graphic above[6], you can see the dramatic increase in effectiveness in bombing accuracy that pilots experience as a result of the intensive training they receive at the TOP GUN school. ***You can also see what happens over time to the skills of the pilots if they are unable to use and practice the newly acquired skills that they have learned. Over time, without reinforcement and practice, their skill level often drops back down to where it was prior to the training.*** This highlights the fact that your training needs to become an ongoing part of what you do on a periodic basis to make sure that the skills and techniques that you have been taught "stick" and become a part of your ongoing behavior.

To keep maintain their skills, TOP GUN graduates are encouraged to practice and teach the techniques that they learned in the TOP GUN school to other pilots in the fleet.

---

6 Report of the Defense Science Board. US Department of Defense. Training Superiority and Training Surprise January 2001.

So how can you easily use and retain the information that you have learned in this book?

Your "go-orders" are to complete each of the steps below in 1-week increments. What I want you to focus on is just testing out, using and applying a minimum of 1 new skill or idea each week. If you want to do more than this, great. On the weekend before each week starts, I want you to block off at least 45 minutes to re-read the appropriate chapter. Do this in a place where you will not be distracted. Doing this in a home office or a private study would be ideal. Make sure to disconnect any phone in the room and turn off your cell phone or pager.

I recommend that at a minimum, you complete the "7 steps" listed below in the order listed. (If you have already accomplished one or more of the steps, so much the better.)

1. Read the Introduction and Chapter one again and take some time to understand the opportunity available in the retirement income planning market. Think carefully about how this marketplace will shape your business during the next decade and beyond. Consider whether you are pushing products to prospects-or working with prospects on creating **planning** solutions. **Take the Quick Quiz and Complete the Knowledge Application test** at the end of Chapter One to gain a better understanding of how to apply the content you learned, your strengths as an individual and what may be holding you back from reaching the next level of success.

2. **Understand the power of branding, positioning and 'share of mind' in creating and differentiating your own personal brand in the marketplace.** You need to understand, use and apply what many of the most successful FORTUNE 500 companies know about the concept of branding and product positioning and creating unconscious associations or linkages between desired emotional states that prospects and clients have and the products and services that you offer. Most importantly, you need to know how to position yourself and what you do in the most favorable way—and to be able to communicate clearly why someone should do business with you rather than the competition. Review Chapter Two and complete the exercises at the end of the chapter to refresh your knowledge of branding and positioning.

3. **Create Your Personal Role Statement** and **Personal Biography brochure.** Remember, your personal role statement is a quick concise explanation of what you do and how you add value. The purpose of a good role statement is to quickly communicate what you do in a powerful and memorable manner. Follow the formula outlined in Chapter Three to create a powerful role statement. Once you understand what a role statement is, follow the formula to create a minimum of three role statements that you can use and test out with live prospects. Regarding your personal biography, make sure it clearly explains to clients what your qualifications and credentials are and how your skills are a match for the needs and wants of your target customers. Review the sample biographies (via the internet web links) that are used by leading military, governmental and business leaders. For your personal biography, you may want to consider creating slightly different biographies depending on whom you will be meeting with. The outline on what to include in your personal biography near the end of Chapter Three will help you get started. Talk to your marketing or compliance people about the best way to get your personal biography 'professionally' produced for use with clients.

4. **Understand and learn how to apply database-marketing techniques to your own book of business.** Conduct the exercise in Chapter Four to identify your best customers so that you understand how to apply your time and future sales efforts the right way with the right people so that you can maximize your sales effectiveness. Vow to spend at least 50% of your time contacting your best, most profitable existing clients. Spend the remaining 50% of your time prospecting for people that look just like your best customers (folks who are similar in age, life-stage, core needs, wants and desires, etc.) –people who are currently doing business with your competition. Your to-do step here is to figure out who those best prospects are and then to develop a plan on how you will spend more 'face-time' in front of prospects and clients that fit this profile. Make sure to leverage and take advantage of any database marketing programs that your firm does with current clients and new prospects. Finally, you need to develop

your own three-ring binder of client testimonials from your best customers. The purpose of this 'testimonial' or reference book is to use it with prospects to powerfully communicate the expertise that you have and the value of what you do.

5. Understand the value of proper 'intelligence gathering' both before your first appointment and during the appointment so that you can tailor your presentation to meet the needs and wants of the unique prospect in front of you. Everyone is driven by different emotional needs, wants and desires. Make sure that you connect with the person by not delivering a 'standard' sales pitch to them. Find out their beliefs, values, needs and wants FIRST- and then tailor your presentation to fit these needs and wants. Review and commit to memory the key fact-finding/profiling questions that all top advisors use. Commit to using these questions during your appointments during the next two weeks and see for yourself how powerful and effective they can be in advancing the sales process.

6. Before you walk in the door to your appointments you should have scripted out a rough outline of what you want to accomplish in the appointment interaction. Not every appointment should result in a sale. You need to know what your goals are for each appointment as well as have a 'fallback goal' of the next best outcome you would like to achieve in the appointment absent a sale. You should clearly understand the power of **scripting** and most importantly how to use **scripting and story selling** concepts to energize and bring to life the customer interaction in a way that adds emotional impact and creates a positive impression on the prospect.

7. Read the examples of scripting and story selling and spend some time developing your own sales scripts and your own sales stories from you past personal experiences. Then use these scripts and stories with real customers to test their effectiveness. Keep the ones that work, discard the others and continue building your own personal script/story-selling book or binder of best practices.

To assist you in applying what you have learned and to better help you apply it in a systematic fashion, feel free to write me at the address listed at the end of the book and I will provide you with access and a password for a complementary, private web site that will provide you with additional examples of role statements, biographies, testimonials, and scripting/story selling sales ideas. A section of the web site will also expand on many of the key topics of this book in greater detail. This private web site is only available to people that purchase this book.

REMEMBER, SUCCESS LEAVES CLUES

Throughout this book you have read example after example that illustrates the mental mindset and the specific strategies that you should use and apply to maximize your own personal performance and sales effectiveness. Remember, there is an "easy way" and a "hard way" to do everything in life. The easy way, outlined in this book, is to use the ideas, best practices and strategies that have been developed and tested successfully over many years to quickly build relationships with customers and prospects that will lead to increased sales activity on your part. You don't need to reinvent the wheel and start from scratch. If something has been proven to work in the past then use it, don't analyze it to death. The information in this book is like a recipe. The recipe may have taken many years to develop and refine to perfection, but now that the recipe is down on paper; ANYONE can use it to produce similar results in a very short period of time. You don't have to spend years creating the recipe; you can just follow the instructions and enjoy the results.

Let me share a final story with you that I heard recently. A long time ago in a place far from where you sit today there was a tiny village that was cursed by a monster. This monster blocked the only road leading out of the village. Many courageous knights sought to fight the monster and kill it with the latest weapons available. The monster, however, possessed a magical power that enabled him to match any weapon he was attacked with and respond with a weapon that was twice as powerful. One fearless Knight attacked the monster with a heavy club but the monster flattened the Knight with a club that was twice as heavy. Another Knight approached from the side and attacked the monster with a heavy sharp sword, but the Knight was cut in two by a sword that was twice as sharp. A third Knight shot a series of flaming arrows at the monster, who replied in turn by unleashing a wall of flame that was twice as hot - incinerating the valiant Knight where he stood. After the failure of the three Knights, the rest of the townspeople decided to stop attacking the monster and attempted to live with him- but they tried to avoid him at all cost.

One day, a child turned up missing from the village. An alarm was sounded and the crowd rushed out to the road where the monster was, fearing the worst. What they saw shocked and amazed them. A little boy was standing in front of the huge monster. The monster reared up on his hind legs and opened his mouth bearing his huge awful teeth. The child smiled innocently at the monster and held up a shiny red apple to him. The monster snarled, sniffed at the apple and gently took it out of the boy's outstretched open hand. The monster ate the apple and then with a roar it slammed it's fist on the ground with tremendous force and instantly two shiny, red, delicious apples appeared that were twice as good as the original apple that the boy offered. The monster gave the apples to the boy. The boy then brought the monster water in a small bucket - and the monster slammed his fist on the ground and magically a golden flask appeared, and in it was juice that was twice as flavorful as the water. The crowd witnessing this event ran back to the village to share this story with anyone who would listen. Before long, others brought gifts to the monster and received a gift back in kind that was twice as good as the one offered. Soon, all the villagers saw the monster for what he really was -a gift and an asset as opposed to a curse. The village and the monster lived happily ever after.

By using and applying the tools, techniques, strategies and best practices that you have learned in this book, just like the boy in the story above, you will be able to connect with, create rapport with and build relationships with even the most fearsome and difficult prospects. When you give your expertise and time freely to existing clients and prospects, by giving value first and positioning yourself, your company and your products the right way, you will almost always get a long-term return that is twice as big as the effort that you put out.

With the right mental mindset and the proper application of the tools of influence, you will be able to create magic in much the same way that the little boy received the two red, shiny apples. People, just like monsters, can be difficult to understand and get to know at first- especially when they think you are trying to sell them something. But when you approach them with an open palm - thinking about their needs and wants first- instead of approaching them with a raised sword or a large club of your needs and wants- magic can happen and you can build relationships for life.

In the beginning of the book, I shared a story with you about one of the greatest salesman in history, Christopher Columbus. He was a master of relationship based selling. He understood the value and importance of having a mission, developing a plan and overcoming adversity on a daily basis. He knew about the power of focus and the importance of having beliefs that would support him. He understood that to become a success he would have to take risks, try new things and above all, he would have to take action and set sail into unfamiliar territory.

In a sense, that's what you have been doing while you read through this book.

I hope that as a result of this book, a light has been turned on in you and a new world of selling has opened up before you.

Remember, the vast majority of people in the world are being persuaded- often without their conscious awareness- by politicians and their armies of political consultants, by savvy marketers, by entrepreneurs and business owners and of course by salespeople.

By using and applying the information presented in this book in an ethical way to build relationships and create customers for life, you can take immediate control of your future, of your career and of your life.

Become one of the elite at what you do and use your new talents, skills and passion for what you do to become twice as good as you are today.

I wish you luck on your future missions!

Enjoy your flight --and live with passion!
Scott Magnacca
Boston, Massachusetts
2012

Contact the Author
Write to
Scott Magnacca
#3 Virginia Drive
Boston, Massachusetts 01757
Or call
508-478-9592
Email: sm.1965@hotmail.com